FROM MANJUNATH TO MANJAMMA

Celebrating
30 Years of Publishing
in India

FROM MANJUNATH TO MANJAMMA

the inspiring
life of a
transgender
folk artist

B. MANJAMMA JOGATHI

WITH HARSHA BHAT

HarperCollins *Publishers* India

First published in India by HarperCollins *Publishers* 2023
4th Floor, Tower A, Building No. 10, DLF Cyber City,
DLF Phase II, Gurugram, Haryana – 122002

2 4 6 8 10 9 7 5 3 1

P-ISBN: 978-93-5699-125-5
E-ISBN: 978-93-5699-112-5

Typeset in 12.5/16 Adobe Caslon Pro at
Manipal Technologies Limited, Manipal

Printed and bound at
Replika Press Pvt. Ltd.

To Matha Kalavva Jogathi who, as my mother and teacher,
taught me this art of Jogathi nritya

To my entire community

To all the readers who will pick up this book and go
through my life's journey

Contents

Preface

I was a woman in a man's body. And ever since I have known this aspect of my being, my life has been a constant struggle. Firstly coming to terms with it myself, then getting people to accept me as I am. The third, which has been ongoing for over four decades now, is to ensure that those like myself and I can live as humans and not as aberrations who disturb those that wish the world were all black and white. And even if I may not have completely succeeded, with my latest achievement, the Padma Shri award that I received from the Government of India, I think I have at least brought our community and its struggles into the mainstream.

This has been possible not because of activism but because of art. This art of ours called Jogathi nritya has empowered many transgenders like me to earn a living,

Preface

to not have to resort to begging or sex work, to gain respect and recognition as folk artists and free ourselves from the clutches of ridicule that the world imprisons us in.

I was once homeless and orphaned just for being true to myself. Today, the same truth has made me a mother to countless sons and daughters who call me Amma and embrace me as their own. Had I been born a man I couldn't have fathered that many, nor could I have given birth to so many had I been a woman.

But my art has ensured I have the privilege and comfort of being 'Amma' to countless children across the globe. And the co-author of this book, Harsha, is now one among them as our bond has grown during the course of over eight months since we first met in Delhi when I received the Padma Shri in November 2021. We have laughed and cried and spoken for hours at length. And together, through endless conversations, we have put together a narrative that seeks to give a glimpse into my life and the world of Jogathis.

Our only effort is to enable inclusive acceptance of those like me by sharing our struggles, our pain, our joys, our fears, and making you, the reader, a part of who I am.

1
Padma Shri

Born: B. Manjunath Setty

Then: Manjamma Jogathi

Now: Padma Shri Maata B. Manjamma Jogathi

The first was an identity of birth, the second of divinity and the third of dignity.

Padma Shri, the fourth-highest civilian award bestowed by the Government of India, although not a title, is the latest addition to my name. This new identity, and the honour and recognition that came with it, transformed not just my life but also the lens through which the world now looks at me and the likes of us—transgenders.

From being loved and caressed as a boon for being born a boy to being called a curse and thrown out by the same parents for turning into a daughter, from being raped and feeling suicidal as a teenager to being a mother and motivation for countless lives, from having nowhere to go and wandering meaninglessly to being invited almost every single day to a new event and being honoured wherever I go, from being no one's Manju to becoming everyone's Manjamma, my life has indeed been a paradigm of paradoxes.

As I reflect on all that has gone by in this almost five-decade-long battle for acceptance, I see it as a battle not just of transgenders but of all those who wish to stand up for their uniqueness, who seek to go beyond their own limitations. It is a battle for identity and inclusion; above all, it is a battle for love and respect. A battle that has been going on for centuries across the world, but one that, fortunately, has the armour or the immunity of culture in this land that has made space within its womb for all of us who, elsewhere, would remain outcasts.

Had I given up due to being a victim, I would probably have become just another entry in the country's record of births and deaths. But I didn't. Perhaps the divine that manifested itself as the dance of life didn't let me die. Else, there would be no tale to tell—the tale of transformation of my being and the world around, the tale of a transgender who danced her way to find for herself and her kind the love, respect and recognition they deserve in a world that truly couldn't care less. The tale of a transgender from a remote corner of Karnataka, whose art became her identity, her survival toolkit, and the wand that broke the dark spell of gloom on the community. No activism could have earned me and my community what my art form—Jogathi nritya—and its pursuit have.

Thanks to this cultural heirloom that I inherited from my first teacher, Matikallu Basappa, and my guru and mother in this commune, Kalavva Jogathi, I can dare to tell this tale as a success story. It's not a story of rags to riches; rather it is a story of a 'pavement to President's court'.

Never did I imagine that an award would turn my life around in this fashion. But it has. It has earned me the love and respect of people across the world. It has managed to finally provide me a roof over my head. At the age of sixty-four, and after almost five decades of being homeless, I have finally secured a home.

Named after my guru mother Kalavva Jogathi, my little nest was made possible thanks to all the generous donors who contributed to it after the national honour made me a household name across the country and in various parts of the world. Which is also why the first thing I placed in this new house—in the room on the first floor that we have built to keep all my awards— is the large maroon-and-golden frame that encases the award certificate signed by the then President of India, Ram Nath Kovind, dated 9 November 2021.

That is a day I hadn't ever dreamt of. I hadn't thought that a simple act of 'taking drishti' of President Kovind—the act of warding off the evil eye as is the tradition among Jogathis—would turn my award reception into a rage on social media, with most people taking pride in my display of our earthy, rustic ways of wishing someone well. It was the perfect finale to the long- awaited award saga, news of which I had first dismissed as a prank.

Yes, when I first received the call about the award, I was in a remote corner of Karnataka holding a training camp for women organized by the Karnataka Folk Academy. I am the first transgender folk artist to be president of this academy and ever since I took charge I have been doing whatever is possible to facilitate the changes I have wished for throughout my struggle as an artist. One such change was to stay on the same premises as the participating folk artists for the duration of the camp, and not just for a day as a token gesture. So, I was in a school in a village in Honnavara, where we were holding a training camp for women artists. I got a call from Delhi, and the girl at the other end asked, '*Aap Manjamma Jogathi ho* (Are you Manjamma Jogathi)?'

While I understand Hindi, I am not very fluent in the language and hence said, '*Haan maa, haan maa* (Yes maa, yes maa).'

'*Aapko Padma Shri award mil gaya* (You have got the Padma Shri award),' said that girl.

I said 'Wrong number' and cut the call. Surely one of our folks must be up to some prank, knowing that I don't know Hindi well, I thought, as I looked at the phone. What confirmed my doubt was the fact that the caller didn't call back. Which is also why I didn't bother telling anyone about this and went about the training sessions as usual.

But that evening, once again there was a call and this time a man asked if I was Manjamma Jogathi, to which I said, '*Hoon ji, Manjamma Jogathi hoon* (Yes, sir, I am Manjamma Jogathi).' He then told me that the Central government had decided to bestow on me the Padma Shri award for my contribution to the field of art.

'Why will they give me the Padma Shri?' I wondered so I just said, '*Theek hai, theek hai* (Okay, okay)', and cut the call since I didn't know what else to say.

He called back again and asked why I cut the call. I said there was some disturbance in the line. The man then asked me for my English biodata. I told him: '*Mereko Hindi barabar nahi aata iske liye main aapko department ka number deta hoon, uske saath baat karo* (I don't know much Hindi, so I am giving you the department phone number, talk to someone there).' They agreed and then took all the details and photographs from our registrar.

But when I called the registrar, they said they had not got any information about the award. So I said, 'Okay, forget it. We didn't seek it anyway. Also, why will they give a Padma Shri to someone like me?' and forgot about it. Those awards, as far as I knew, were given only to big and accomplished artists, actors, scientists, businesspeople, sportspeople. I didn't know they would give it to folk artists. Moreover, I hadn't heard about the Padma Shri award until they gave it to Saalumarada

Thimmakka, the tree warrior. I had only known of the Padma Bhushan and Padma Vibhushan because Dr Rajkumar, the famous Kannada actor who was once kidnapped by sandalwood smuggler Veerappan, had been awarded the former. I knew these were big awards, but I didn't know they were given by the Central government. Because when Dr Rajkumar received it, newspapers and the like were not part of our lives; we have been reading newspapers only in the last ten-fifteen years or so. They had by then started flashing the news on all television channels, apparently.

I returned to my room in the evening. Had there been a bed in the school I would have stayed back with the participants, since everything was really pleasant there. But since I find it difficult to get up if I sleep on the floor, I stayed in a hotel nearby, to which I would retire post dinner, which all of us would have together.

That day, I had worn a white saree petticoat, which I intended to use again two days later for another saree. Inside the room it would take two days to dry, unlike in the open, so I thought I would wash it that night and it would be ready for the day after. Thinking this way, I changed into a kurta and headed to wash my clothes. But since I couldn't squat on the floor, I sat on the Western lavatory and got to washing. It was then that I heard my phone ringing continuously. I began to wonder what kind of people would call so incessantly and why they wouldn't get that if someone didn't answer once, it meant the person was busy. Do people lack even such basic sense? I thought to myself as the phone kept ringing. I also began to get angry, wondering what kind of people lacked the basic sense to wait for a few minutes.

I rose from the seat, washed the soap off my hands and wiped them on the kurta I was wearing, and headed to pick up the phone since I was alone in the room. It was the academy registrar. I wondered why this lady was calling at this hour. I called her back and she said, '*Amma, abhinandanegalu* (Amma, congratulations).'

'Why, maa?'

'Amma, we just got the information at the academy also. Congratulations, Amma. We are very happy, Amma,' she said.

As I was talking to her, I saw the announcement on television. As the news sunk in, I cut the call, only to have a barrage of callers congratulate me. Everyone was wishing me and saying things, most of which I wasn't even able to make sense of at that moment. My hands and feet began to tremble as there was no one there to share that moment of joy.

There were 188 missed calls on my phone. I spoke to people till 1 a.m. that night until my phone finally shut down. I then left it to charge and went back to wash the skirt. After that I checked WhatsApp on my other phone, a smartphone. There were more than 700 unread messages. A storm of wishes struck me and I sat awake the whole night responding to them. It was 6 a.m. by the time I finished responding to each of those heartfelt wishes with gratitude—for that was all I could give in return for all the love I was receiving.

Finally that phone too gave up and I put it to charge and picked up the 'keypad' phone to see 198 missed calls. That's when I realized that these many people had called me the previous night as I kept answering calls. But I couldn't see who all had called since the keypad phone doesn't show details beyond ten callers. I felt bad for not knowing who the others were that I couldn't respond to.

That morning I decided to first get ready and then switch the two phones on, since otherwise I would have no time for anything but receiving calls. I took a shower and got ready, switched on the smartphone and called back all those whose calls I had missed until I reached the school where the training was being held. Once there, I realized all the media people and reporters had been ringing up and asking, 'Where is Manjamma, where is Manjamma, her phone is switched off, where is Manjamma … We have been trying all night, where is Manjamma?' They only knew I had gone to some training camp, but no one except the academy staff knew of my whereabouts. They had then contacted the academy, taken the contact details of the school and then, knowing that I was in Honnavara, deputed their local reporters to the school.

'It is your fortune that our Manjamma is in your town,' the school folk are said to have told the reporters from Honnavara who then landed up at the school and began to do interviews and honour me for the award. The school folk shared that earlier too, people who had been visiting had similarly been announced as recipients for the Rajyotsava and Padma Shri awards. It was the 'sthala mahime' (glory of the place) of that village, they said with glee, and they were proud that this one had come my way while I was at their school.

We went back to our training sessions and I attended the countless calls and interviews at the venue itself as I didn't want to head back to Bengaluru midway. 'If it was anyone else, they would have straightaway headed to Bengaluru, Amma, and basked in the glory of all the media attention sitting in the offices of news channels, Amma, but you aren't even getting back to the academy,' said a few who called.

'How can I head back?' I asked them. How could I abandon those young artists, those young women whose parents had trusted their girls with me, thinking Amma was around and would take care of them like a mother. For me, that responsibility was huge; I couldn't leave them midway, and hence stayed back for the next three days and only then headed back to Bengaluru.

All the villagers kept saying that it was strange for them to see me there amongst them even after the award announcement. I was astonished hearing this; it felt only natural that I do what had made me worthy of the award in the first place—be committed to my art.

But for months on end since I returned to Bengaluru, my days were spent attending countless felicitation events. Wherever I went, people would come and pay their respects and honour me. Whether I was at the office or at home, there would be someone or the other who turned up to 'sanmaana' and invite me to various places to be felicitated.

The award wasn't there as yet. The ceremony was delayed for a long time owing to the pandemic. But the honour that followed the announcement was doubled with all the delay. When it was almost a year, though, people started asking, 'Amma, when are they giving you the prashasti? The announcement was made in November and another November has gone by; they spoke about it last January but another January is here.'

'Kotre kodli, bitre bidli (If they give, let them give, if they don't, let them not). People have already given me the Padma Shri. They have already started addressing me as Padma Shri Manjamma Jogathi now, so whether they give or not, it doesn't really matter,' I would remark, as the awards and honours I had received since the announcement were far too many in the waiting period.

'Why do you worry?' I would ask, since the honour of the award had already been prefixed to my name. Each time I would say that it's okay even if they didn't give me the award, I had people trying to explain, 'It's a different honour, Amma.'

'But where do I go ask them for the award if they aren't giving it yet? I don't know English or Hindi. With my Kannada, where shall I go to enquire, when are you giving me the award?' The silence that would follow was of cluelessness cloaked in jest.

Finally, on 15 October, a letter arrived at the academy saying that the award ceremony was to be held on 8 November. So, on the night of 6 November, I left from my house, a tin-sheet-roofed two-room space that I have been calling home for decades, in Mariyammanahalli, for Bengaluru airport. Along with the academy superintendent Prakash and my god-given son Vikram, I was to fly to Delhi on the morning of the seventh. I asked Vikram to join as I needed someone who could speak English.

The flight to Delhi was like a carnival of emotions because to begin with, it was my maiden flight experience and that too to receive one of the nation's highest honours. Second, it was the post-pandemic phase, which meant a lot of COVID protocols had to be followed. The COVID test had to be done at the airport. I could feel the jitters since I hadn't ever been tested until then. I had been touring so many districts but never got tested since I believed I had been following all the safety measures.

But for Delhi, it was mandatory and all of us would have to get tested. Prakash had recovered from COVID. Vikram had got himself tested multiple times since he's a frequent flyer, so he was casual. Prakash and I were both worried. We got tested and the hours that followed were the most uneasy. What if we tested positive? Who would then receive the Padma Shri? What if the results were declared positive upon reaching Delhi? Where then would they put us up for quarantine? They told us the results would be delivered on the phone and the sight of the phone since that moment began to feel like a ticking explosive. We kept uttering random things to each other, talking for talking's sake, but it hardly helped calm our minds.

Trying to distract ourselves, we opened the packed dosas, one each for us, that Vikram had carried from Bengaluru, as food at the airport, he had told me, was very expensive. But that was not filling enough and I asked him to fetch some idlis. When he turned up with a plate of breakfast—three idlis and one vada—I asked him how much it cost, since he had mentioned that the airport doesn't have inexpensive eating options.

'Two hundred and eighteen rupees, Amma,' said Vikram. My heart skipped a beat. 'Three idlis for two hundred rupees!' Vikram reminded me that this was the airport and that's how it was here.

'Vikram, if four idlis cost one rupee, how many idlis would we get for 218 rupees?' I asked him. Way back in 1986 I used to sell idlis to make ends meet and would go out into the city with a box of 3-4 kg of idli and chutney and sell four idlis for one rupee. To eat idlis worth 218 rupees was truly beyond my imagination.

After this, when we finally boarded the flight, I had butterflies in my stomach. I was scared throughout because I kept wondering about all the possibilities, especially with the test results. Finally we landed. And the moment the flight came to a halt, I wanted to click a picture with the pilot because this man had flown us in the skies with care and attention and landed us safely at our destination. He was God for me at that moment, because this effort for me was no less than any superhuman task. Humans today can accomplish what in earlier times was a skill or possibility reserved for the gods alone.

I told Vikram I would like to have a picture with that God who flew me across the skies for the first time. Vikram went to ask the airhostesses and told them about my award, that it was my maiden flight and of my wish to thank the pilot. They went and enquired and then he agreed to meet, but not for a picture initially. He later obliged but asked us not to share the images on social media and the like.

Fortunately for us, the COVID reports were negative upon landing. When we reached Ashoka Hotel, whichever way I turned in the lobby, I saw Manjamma. It was surreal, almost dream-like, to see posters of myself all around a hotel that looked palatial.

We went to the room, rested for the day and the next morning woke up to get ready. In the bathroom were half-a-dozen bottles with soap, shampoo and all else.

Which of these was for the hand, the hair, the body? I began to wonder what to do with all these bottles. I looked around and realized there was no bucket, no jug. How was one to have a bath in this bathroom, I wondered. There was a large tub in one corner, though— the kind they show in films. In that too I could only find the place from where the water was to drain out. But I couldn't figure out how to use it or where water came into it from.

So I came out and gave Vikram a call, asking him how on earth one was one to have a bath. He told me to turn the tap to the left for hot, right for cold and centre for water to pour down from the top. You have to stand under it and take a shower, he said. I asked him how to stand and bathe as I was not used to it. 'You have to have a bath like that only, Amma, there's no provision to sit,' he said.

Fine, I thought, and headed back to that strange bathroom and as I sifted through the multiple bottles, began to once again wonder what bottle served what purpose. What if I use the one for the hair for the face or something else somewhere else? What if I use it wrongly and my skin peeled off or I had some allergic reaction? If something were to go wrong, who would go collect the Padma Shri? All those names were in English and were confusing. Not wanting to risk using any of these, I pushed them all aside, wore my saree skirt and went back to the room to fetch my own soap and shampoo and took a shower. Then I headed out. It was 8

November. We went to to the venue, where they trained us on how to walk, stand and receive the award. Then we went back to the room.

On the day of the award ceremony, 9 November, I awaited my turn. My serial number was 21. I simply stood watching all the others walk up, receive their awards and head back, and the President greet all of them. As I was watching him sit and rise to honour each one, I felt bad that he, at this age, had to tire himself out this way. Isn't this exercise hurting him, he looks old, must be getting tired, I thought.

It then struck me that if we were at any such gathering and tired ourselves out, our mother would show us love and take drishti to rid us of the weariness. Maybe I should do the same for the President, I thought. When my turn came, I went and did namaskar to the steps and waved my veil once. I think the President was taken aback so he remained one step back and looked at what I was doing. As I waved the veil once again, he asked me, '*Yeh kya hai* (What is this)?'

'*Aapko teen din se nazar hui hai, is ke liye main nazar nikali* (You've been the object of the evil eye for three days, that's why I am warding it off),' I told him.

'*Oh, shukriya, theek hai, theek hai* (Oh, thank you, okay),' he said.

And that was it. A simple, genuine act of mine went viral and people from across the world began to talk about it and share the visuals. The entire media went gaga over it.

Because it was an act of pure love and concern, an act that most mothers in my country perform, believing firmly in the power of intention to clear anything that could possibly bring the other person harm, an act that has its roots in the tradition of wishing well for the other, and beyond all an act traditionally seen as being even more auspicious when performed by transgenders, an act that is not superstition but almost a mini superpower.

The following day the Karnataka Kala Sangha had arranged for a felicitation event, which I attended and then returned to Bengaluru. Upon landing, there was a felicitation at the MGM College and they also booked a big hotel. When I told them to book a regular hotel, they said, 'No, Amma, you have to listen to us, it is our honour,' they said. 'You can't stay in a normal hotel.' Here I was, having had enough of one big hotel and its bathroom for two days, wishing I didn't have to go through it all over again!

They insisted and said, 'You are stepping into Karnataka after receiving such a big honour, so we want to ensure the best of hospitality', while I began to mentally fret at the impending honour of this 'best' hospitality.

How was I to tell them my woes with the 'bucketless' bathroom and its carnival of bottles? They booked me yet again into another big hotel—I can't remember its name—only for me to find those bottles again. This time I called Vikram and asked him what was what and then took a shower.

When the principal of the college visited me, and I showed him that flute-like award cover. He asked me what was in it. I told him it was the Padma Shri certificate and he asked if he could touch it. 'By all means,' I said.

After seeing it, he requested if they could frame it themselves and present it to me once again at the college. 'Else it may simply get torn, with visitors seeking to have a look at it, just like us,' he reasoned and I agreed. They got it framed and hosted a wonderful event and felicitated me, and I returned home as 'Padma Shri B. Manjamma Jogathi'.

It sits today in this house it has earned for me and my fellow Jogathis, so we can live as well as die in peace and with dignity, with a roof over our heads.

2

From Manju to Manjamma—Discovering the Woman Within

It was certainly not easy but it was what I wanted—to be a woman. I was born a boy but never felt like one. And as all transgender women whose tales have been told so far will explain, the woman in us is seated deep within and she emerges untamed, graceful and seeking to be accepted in full blood and flesh. The kind of 'bhava' or emotion predominant in the feminine force is what most defines our journey thereon.

Within me, the key quality or feeling has always been to be caring, nurturing warmth and the instinct to take responsibility for others in the classic Indian definition of motherhood. The same concern drove me to strive for my community through this art form and made me ward off the evil eye from the President. The 'amma' appended to my name is not just a gender-altering suffix; it defines my very personality.

As I have already said, I was born B. Manjunath Setty, a name that stayed with me for just eighteen years of my life. I was one among the twenty-one children my mother chose to bear, of whom only four survived—two sisters, an older brother and I. We had another brother whom we lost to cancer at the age of twenty-one.

We come from a village named Kallukamba in the Bellary district of Karnataka but I didn't grow up there. My father changed many jobs, hence I really can't call any town my own. Also, as a Jogathi, a transgender, we have no place we can call our own. We live a nomadic life, moving from one place to another, singing and seeking alms, performing and telling tales.

I was born in Kampli where my father was working in a factory; when I was five years old my father got a job at the Birla factory in Harihara. In Harihara, our house was on the bank of a river and as children we would build huts and play 'house-house'. My mother told me later that even then, I always liked to play a girl and the homemaker.

I can't forget the joy with which my mother used to dress me up as Shri Krishna; there's even a photograph which I treasure. On my first day at school, she dressed me up as Shri Krishna, hair in a topknot, wearing chains made of mandakki, fluffy rice and seeds, and so on. She even held a little ritual and distributed a sweet mixture of coconut and jaggery to the other children to announce her Krishna's first day at school. But to her misfortune, her Krishna did not exist for long; he grew up to be Brihannala, the transgender form that Arjuna assumes during the Pandavas' exile period.

My father was very proud of his hardworking son who would bring his lunch to the factory even as a schoolboy. However, that too was short-lived. It vanished when the woman within me wrestled her way to claim my body and my being. Although she had always been inside me and gave glimpses of her strong hold over my body and behaviour, it was only when I was in, say, Class 7, that the feminine within began to be more and more evident.

While some say it is a sort of abnormality, in our part of the country, especially in the northern districts of Karnataka, it is seen as our lives being taken over by the Goddess we worship. It is her tale, the tale of Yellamma, that we as Jogathis dedicate our lives to telling by singing, dancing and seeking alms. It is through her grace that the feminine power chooses to manifest through us and that is how we in northern Karnataka see ourselves too—as an embodiment of the divine.

The turmoil within, though, is beyond description and I wish it upon none else. The pain is something that can't be shared with anyone else. They are not the feelings of coming of age, of a boy turning into a man or a girl into a woman. The emotions are neither of a boy, nor a girl, and can't be shared with either. I didn't really feel welcome among the boys or the girls.

I couldn't make friends with boys since I would feel shy to talk to them, nor did I feel like I belonged among them or was one of them. Whenever I would try to talk to them, they would shoo me away saying I didn't belong as I was 'acting like a girl' and it made them uncomfortable and embarrassed. 'We are boys and you aren't like one of us. So you should stay away from us, it is embarrassing. People will start talking ill about us and probably create stories about our association with you. Please stay away,' they would say.

I yearned to talk to my female classmates but didn't dare to. On the few occasions I did, they would keep their distance. Not like I could blame them. I was, after all, a boy, I dressed like one. They would smirk at my gait that was beginning to appear feminine. They would talk among themselves, wondering why I acted like a girl at times and wanted to be with them. My talk, my walk, my expressions, my emotions and the way they manifested physically in terms of my body language were all feminine.

Despite the awkwardness, I still wished to hear them talk, to be like them and share my feelings with them. I wanted to tell them I was like them, I felt like them. But how was I to do this? They wouldn't accept me. They saw me as a boy, but I knew I didn't feel like one. I was a woman in my understanding of myself—the feminine gentleness within, the motherly nature of caring and taking responsibility for household tasks reserved for women back then, my feminine way of viewing the world, while on the physical plane too the way I walked, sat, moved and behaved was very womanly.

It wasn't girly, it was womanly. What I mean is that I began to imitate my mother, wear a towel across my chest the way she would drape her saree pallu, draw a rangoli in front of the house after waking up, help with the cooking and wash vessels after we were done eating, do pooja even at the cost of getting yelled at by my mother day in and day out. It was an inexplicable situation both within myself and for those around me.

I must have been around twelve or thirteen years old at the time. It started when I was, say, in Class 7 but the feelings intensified when I was in Class 9. At the same time, people around me began to sense a feminine side emerge more prominently in my way of being.

My tryst with the stage and of playing a character beyond the dualities of gender too began then. When I was in Class 7, we staged a drama called *Thiruneelakantha* in school. At that time women didn't take part in dramas; men would shave off their facial hair and play female roles. Our teacher, Basappa Master, offered me the role of Paramatma, God himself. But since he was organizing the play and was one of the first to be sensitive to my changing self and feminine emotions, he also had in mind another role for me.

'Will you dance as a girl?' he asked. I wasted no time agreeing. It was clearly what I wished to do, what I longed to experience—to dress like a girl, to dance like one, to be seen as one.

After I was done playing my Paramatma role in the play, I changed into a skirt and full-sleeved blouse and danced like there was no one watching. The feel of the skirt around my waist inspired me to dance with a zeal and joy I hadn't known before. Basappa Master announced my name as Bengaluru Lata and I danced, swaying and moving like a girl. I was overjoyed with the way the audience responded.

And that was, in many ways, the beginning of my dance of destiny.

Every time I saw someone dance sporting women's clothes, I too would be motivated to see myself don a braid, a blouse and skirt, and dance unapologetically. But I couldn't do this at home; at times I was even beaten up by my father. So, I would wait to be alone; then I would wear women's clothes and admire myself.

For the next three years after the first play, any female roles in programmes in school were mine—unsaid, unasked. That brought this side of me to greater notice; this in turn strengthened my desire to be a woman. When something is no longer hidden, it eventually stops crippling you from within and instead becomes your strength.

I had begun to feel like a woman in every aspect of my being, but how was I to explain it anyone? I stopped hanging out with the boys or playing with them, for I would often feel shy when I saw them. Nor did I seek the company of the girls in class. I chose solitude over the sense of not belonging that I experienced in either instance.

It was around the same time, in Class 8 or 9, that I began to get seizures and epileptic attacks, often even foaming at the mouth. Doctors said all was fine. Astrologers and priests said it was the Goddess who was making me go through all this, seeking submission. My parents refused to buy that argument.

'He is doing all this intentionally, best to ignore it. He will be fine,' they said and let things be as they were. How were they to know any better? How was I to tell them it was something unfolding deep within?

I intensified my worship and pooja at home; at the same time my mother completely stopped involving herself in them. People began to gossip that the Goddess was beginning to take over my life. Whatever it was, it began to take a toll on my body and mind; I couldn't focus on my studies and in the Class 10 board exams I failed in English and science. My father decided there was no sense in my pursuing academics and packed me off to Kallukamba, our ancestral village, where my brother had moved after his studies and set up a kirana or provisions store.

My father had apparently left the village after a fight with his siblings, vowing to return only after his children came of age. He had kept his word and only after my brother had cleared his Class 10 board exams and was old enough to set up shop did my father take him and one of my sisters to Kallukamba, got them settled there and returned to Kukwada, where he worked at the time. I was deputed to help out my brother at the store but I couldn't manage to do any of the tasks he assigned. Once again I chose solitude over the tyranny of being misunderstood even by my own siblings.

Since I wasn't of any help at the store, my brother asked me to instead go on his rounds of payment collection. I would gape at the women and observe them closely, the way they dressed and walked, their mannerisms. I obsessively yearned to be like them, so much so that I would sometimes faint. People began to say that the Goddess Huligemma had begun to take control of my life. This was what people said if a boy started behaving like a woman.

I had begun to worship Huligemma on Tuesdays and Fridays, the days dedicated to goddesses. People saying she had 'entered' me only strengthened my own belief that indeed she had. I would completely lose myself while worshipping her and occasionally even feel possessed.

On one such day, when I was pondering about all that was happening to me, my body and life around me, I felt the sky spin and fell to the floor. The next thing I knew I heard voices; not my own, other voices. People later said I would make pronouncements, clear statements. They were not random words but clairvoyant-like statements. I couldn't remember anything I said. It was a difficult time since I couldn't make sense of all that was happening.

'The Setty boy is being possessed by Huligemma. He is becoming a Jogamma.' This is what people said, and their words began to hurt my family members. It was a matter of disgrace because we belonged to the Aryavaishya community. According to our beliefs, being possessed or having one's life being taken over by goddesses like Yellamma or Huligemma, or becoming a devadasi, were things confined to those belonging to the lower castes, not us.

I wish they had realized that nature doesn't recognize these manmade classifications, nor that it had sought my permission before it made these changes to my body and persona. But they didn't and that got me more abuse. I was bringing disgrace to the community. I was a blot on my caste. And now I had turned into one from a lower caste.

Cut to four decades later and an association of the same community had organized a large event where they wanted me to perform with my troupe and to honour me for my achievements! And the line of persuasion was that I had to make time since I belonged to the community! It was my last full-fledged performance with the whole troupe in recent times, since the artist in me has had to take a back seat after I took over as president of the Karnataka Folklore Academy.

Such are the ways of the world. Life comes full circle in ways never imagined. Those who cringed at the mention of my name now wish to have it inscribed with fanfare. But back then, none of what was being discussed about caste made any sense to me. I was being treated like a criminal, but as far as I knew, I had actually done nothing. What was happening to me was beyond my own will and discretion.

Looking back, it was also beyond the people's wisdom and understanding. They were distraught and did not know what to make of me in our ancestral village. They didn't want me sitting at home with the womenfolk because they felt their company would only make me more 'womanly'. They would pack me off to the fields to work with the boys and that for me was the most torturous experience. On the one hand were my thoughts that left me lost and confused, and on the other was the mockery and name-calling by the boys working in the fields. I don't know which bit hurt more—the verbal torture I had to face all day or the uneasiness I experienced working with them, which was shredding me to bits from within.

I decided to stand up for myself and refused to go to the fields. All hell broke loose. It was as if I had invited the fury of not just my extended family but the entire village. They tied me to a cot and whipped me black and blue. I had brought disrepute to the family and they used all their 'manliness' to ensure I shed my non-manliness and confirmed. Initially, it was my brother who beat me up. Later, my relatives ganged up and many more gathered around to watch. What was most unbearable, worse than the physical abuse, was the sound of their words and the laughter of onlookers.

I would wear trousers and a shirt for the payment collection or to the bank, but at home I always wore a lungi, but never lifted it like the boys did. As with a saree, I ensured it always covered my legs and draped a towel over my bosom. This made me the butt of jokes.

'Hey, speak like a man!' the staff at the bank would say, repeatedly asking me why I spoke like a woman. 'But I have always spoken this way, ever since I was a child,' I would respond. Eventually, they stopped bothering me since I was very efficient with my work and they couldn't care less, although they would whisper every time I was around.

There were always men who would intentionally touch and feel me, and laugh when I reacted. The women, on the other hand, would watch from a distance. Although I would react with a frown to them calling me effeminate, somewhere deep down, I was glad that the feminine within was being recognized and the 'effeminate' tag was more of a title than an abuse. I would be glad that they saw the one I was forced to hide—the woman in me.

After being in Kallukamba for about over a year, my brother eventually gave up beating and yelling as he too realized the futility of it all. Around that time the intensity of feeling possessed also increased. According to the villagers, I apparently would make predictions or pronouncements, good for a few, bad for a few. I don't know; I don't remember. All I know is that the villagers believed the Goddess had possessed me and so my brother sent me back to Kukwada, to our parents.

≈

Upon returning to Kukwada I found, to my surprise, my maternal uncle, Gandhi maava, also at home. Maybe I could get some help from him, I thought, for he too had become a Jogathi. After all the rebuke and abuse I had received from my paternal relatives, I hoped he would understand what I was going through, from his own experience. But that was not to be.

He was furious. He thought he would rid me of the spell of the Goddess somehow and told my parents he would take me to Kampli. What I thought would have been a bond of empathy turned into another wave of inhuman existence. He dismissed everything as drama and beat me to ensure I 'become normal again'. He became my guru later and initiated me into the life of a Jogathi, but for now he was a tyrant who, again in all 'good faith', wished I should not have the life he did.

While all that Manju wanted was to be rid of the struggle within and become Manjamma, Gandhi maava probably knew that it would only mark the beginning of a lifetime of strife. That's why he wanted to reverse what was happening in the present to avoid a devastating future. But he couldn't. All his trashings were futile because an even more turbulent battle raged within me. This woman seated within was unleashing all her powers. She would not let me be. She wanted to be herself through me and tell Manju that he existed only on paper, not in reality.

'This fellow is a loafer and I can't rectify him. Come and take him back,' Gandhi maava told my parents when he could no longer handle my behaviour. He gave up trying to discourage me. Years later, when I stood where he had then, I too initially tried to dismiss those who came to me with similar intentions, telling them all of it was their own doing and they should try to overcome it.

I realized that it was Gandhi maava's pain that was talking, the pain from the penury, the pitiable pursuit of acceptance and the perils on the path. Distanced first by my brother and now my uncle, I headed back home.

Then something happened: I started bleeding, as if I were menstruating. Every month. My undergarments and lungi would be stained with blood but there was no pain. I don't remember how that happened. This went on for a few months. We went to the doctor, did the tests he prescribed, but everything seemed normal. Then it stopped suddenly, on its own. No one knew why. They only knew I was 'strange'.

The priests and elders said this was the Goddess's doing and that my parents should let me go, have me submit to the Goddess, do the 'mutthu kattisikollodu' (getting beads tied) ritual, and become a Jogathi. 'You have lost so many you gave birth to, count this one too among the dead,' they told my mother.

But how was a mother to accept it? This was a mother who had delivered twenty-one children and would have delivered more if my father hadn't managed to con her into getting operated. This was a mother who had cursed and held the government responsible for the death of two of her children, part of the triplets she had delivered. The government had gifted her a cradle as her delivery of triplets back then had been big news. But when first one and then another died, leaving just one alive, she said the government was to blame. 'If only they had gifted three cradles, maybe all three of my Brahma, Vishnu, Eshwar would have survived,' she would say and swear at the government in pain. But even the third one died, at twenty-one, of cancer.

And as fate would have it, she finally had to let go of another son when I chose to no longer be a son but a daughter. My seizures began to increase once I returned from Gandhi maava's place to my parents in Kukwada. Instances of my uttering prophecies also grew.

At the time, it was believed that something bad would happen to anyone who hurts those possessed by the Goddess. On one occasion, upon being insulted, apparently I said that bad news would follow. The following day, my father got news that my sister had fought with my brother in the ancestral village and it had got so bad that she had poured kerosene and set herself on fire.

This incident shook my father and when I began to bleed, he is said to have prayed to the Goddess for a clue that it was indeed Her doing and that She had taken ownership of my life. He held some mud in his hand and proclaimed that if it was indeed the Goddess's doing, the mud should turn into Iobana. If he received indication of this, he himself would have me wear a saree and submit myself to Her.

Once he got 'proof', he agreed to have me submit to the Goddess, but apparently he told my mother he wouldn't let me wear a saree the way Jogathis do. I was unaware of all this but, as my mother told me later, I was 'possessed' that very day and in that state I narrated the discussion they had had.

The very next day, I bled yet again and was hospitalized. This confirmed my father's fears and he decided to take me to Huligi and get the ritual of tying divine beads done. The onslaught of verbal abuses also ceased.

No parent would have willingly enabled a child to take on another gender identity; it was the divinity attached to the whole transformation that made it possible. That's what influenced their decision, however reluctantly, to submit their son to the Goddess, to carry Her name instead of their family's and to let him turn into a woman. They now believed there was no other option but to let the Goddess have Her way.

The following day was the one I had waited for— the day of denouncing my identity as Manju and of becoming Manjamma, Manjamma Jogathi.

3

A New Me—Initiated to Be a Jogathi

It was the turning point of my life—the day I received 'dcckshc' or initiation into the Jogathi order. The world came crashing down for everyone around me, but I felt liberated. On this day I could finally shed the cloak of a gender that had been forced upon me and flaunt what I had always wished to be—a woman.

I would no longer have to stealthily try on women's clothes and check myself out in the mirror. I would no longer have to wear men's clothes as if they were women's clothing. I would no longer have to gaze at women and wish I could also sport flowers, a big bindi, anklets, a blouse, a flowing saree with its pleats falling at my feet, dark-green glass bangles, a sparkling nose stud—none of these would remain on my wish list, they would be part of who I was. I would no longer have to fear for my life, I would no longer be thrashed for sporting any of these symbols of womanhood. Like the time I once was when I was at my Gandhi maava's place. Those episodes of being hunted down and trashed left me scarred for days.

Weeks before my initiation, Gandhi maava told me he was headed to the neighbouring village to seek alms and would return the following day. As soon as he left, I

41

wrapped my lungi like a skirt, put on a shirt and threw the towel gracefully across my bosom like a saree pallu. I looked at myself in the mirror, applied beeswax, which he used as kumkum, on my lips so that they glistened, drew a round bindi on my forehead and wore two press ear studs that I managed to find.

I rummaged through Gandhi maava's padligi, the cane basket that Jogathis use to seek alms, pulled out two rupees, headed out and locked the door behind me. I spread a mattress on the verandah, placed pillows along the length to make it look as if a person was sleeping there, covered them with a sheet and left for the cinema nearby.

I bought myself a balcony ticket using the two rupees, which was a huge amount in those days, and was soon engrossed in the film, *Apoorva Sangama*, especially the leading lady Ambika's appearance, her movements, her clothes and her mannerisms. As I imitated her dance movements sitting in my chair, I was happily lost in a world that I had escaped into. But just as actor Rajkumar started singing '*Tara oh Tara*' and looking for Ambika, my maava turned up at the theatre, looking for me. He had gone home and, finding the door locked, enquired with the neighbours who told him that I had left, all dressed up as a woman. 'Where else could he have gone but to the theatre?' they said.

All the drama with which I had headed to the cinema, the dreamy mood I was in, imagining myself dressed like the heroine, and the romanticism of those feminine movements—everything vanished the moment I saw him.

Gandhi maava had a lit beedi in one hand and a staff in the other, and was hunting for me among the seats below. The screen light shone on him and I could recognize him from his appearance even in the darkness of the cinema hall. He seemed furious as he kept searching and asking people around. He then asked the guards at the gate, 'Have you seen our Manju?' They knew me as the theatre was barely a hundred metres away from our house, and they used to call me 'Gandhiyamma's aliya nephew, or Kwantrajogamma's [another name for Gandhi maava] nephew'. They told him that I had just stepped down from the balcony and left, which only enraged Gandhi maava further.

Meanwhile, I had reached home, wiped off the beeswax kumkum from my lips, and was lying on the mattress pretending to be asleep. Gandhi maava also got home, picked a large wooden stick and began to beat me. He continued to whack me mercilessly. 'You went there to lure the men all dressed up?' he shouted, all the while using the choicest of cuss words that I'm embarrassed to even recall and muttering furiously.

I peed my pants and screamed for help. Hearing my cries so late in the night, neighbours came running to my rescue, fearing I would be killed. An elderly woman who lived next door advised my uncle not to beat me so ruthlessly. 'Look at him, avva (grandmother),' my uncle said. 'He has gone to the theatre dressed like a woman.'

Luckily for me, she tried to calm down my uncle, saying, 'We will ensure he doesn't go out like this in the future.' I shudder to this day thinking of that night; it took me almost three days to recover from the fever I got following the beating. The moment I was better, my uncle said he could no longer host me and dropped me back at my parents'.

However, in a matter of a few weeks, Gandhi maava was present at my initiation; it was he who cut my uddaara, the waist thread, as part of the initiation ceremony. Typically, the person who does this is seen as a mother to the new initiate within the Jogathi community. It was heart-warming for me but must have been heartbreaking for him, for he had tried his best to deter me from this path. But nature had other plans.

The beauty and majesty of this practice that embraces us in a cultural cocoon is that it secures for us what no system or law can. Way before activism could, tradition had secured for us the right to be different yet respected. Long before the modern world could contemplate on a community of those who do not conform to the two polar ends of the gender spectrum, we in our culture did. And in stark contrast to the hijra tradition, which has been documented by many, ours is one in which a sense of community is accompanied by an aura of divinity. This sets us apart; this is also what gave me an opportunity to strive for acceptance characterized by respect, not disdain.

Although there are similarities with other communities of transgenders, we Jogathis are blessed and worshipped, and not forced into prostitution. We are seen as chosen by Goddess Yellamma herself to dedicate our lives to her service as avatars of Parashurama, who takes birth on earth in this form to make up for his sin of having questioned his mother's chastity. There is also the tale of how Rishi Jamadagni's other sons who didn't obey his orders to severe their mother Renuka's head, were cursed by him to be born as 'napunsaka' (neither male nor female). We have our art that enables us to earn both a living and respect.

Which is why, no matter how hard it is for our families, they let go of us to live with our community but don't look down upon us as having committed a crime. Yes, many of us are disowned and cast out for a few years, and that makes life a living hell for us. At least it used to happen back in my younger days, but that's mostly because of a sense of disappointment, of having to give up a son from whom a family has expectations in the naive and innocent sense of the term. But that too can change, and that is the message I have for everyone now—if a child like me is born in your home, accept the situation and give the child an education to empower them to be independent and live a decent life. This empowerment can change everything.

This is what my experience of being rejected, disowned, and then not just accepted but embraced and celebrated by family and people around has been. The moment of transition is traumatic for those who witness it; for instance, my mother couldn't stop cursing the Goddess for having taken her son from her.

Not all parents volunteer to be part of this ceremony, but mine did. For those whose parents wouldn't oblige and who would come to me for help, I would organize the ritual. There are two parts to it: first is the formal ritual of discarding the old identity, not just of gender, but caste, family and all else too. This is called the 'mutthu kattisikollodu', or getting beads tied.

This ceremony was usually performed at the Huligi, Chandraguthi, Savadatti or Ucchangidurga temples, whichever was convenient to travel to. We went to Huligi for my ritual. A priest was assigned the task of this ritual to initiate the man seeking to be a woman as a Jogathi. A priest by the name of Pujara Balappa conducted the rituals for me at the Huligemma temple in Huligi village, Hospet taluk. Later, however,the government banned such rituals at temples and now the priests don't do it any more.

The initiate sits dressed in white while the waist thread, or uddara, which the boy wears since birth, is cut. This symbolizes the end of the identity held so far. Five Jogathis then apply turmeric and give the new initiate a bath, and present a set of new 'female' clothes to change into. Once she is changed, the initiate goes to the priest who hands over five plain beads and two pendants with the faces or the feet of deities marked on them to be strung on a turmeric-stained thread for the initiate to wear. She is also given a padligi or the ceremonial cane casket and a figure of the deity to carry on a pot on her head. The first saree marks the official transition of identity. I remember, as I wrapped this saree around myself, tears began to flow even though I felt deeply content inside. Once the initiate puts on the 'thaali' or mangalsutra, a necklace that married women wear in parts of India, the initiation as a Jogathi is complete. Jogathis wear the thaali all the time after the ceremony.

Although Gandhi maava became my new mother after I was initiated, I never called him Gandhemma, I always addressed him as 'maava'. Most people who know us from childhood do not take to our new names and often call us what they always used to. To this day, many of my classmates call me Manju, 'le', or Setty, as they used to in our childhood.

Gandhi maava's face reflected a sense of helpless acceptance that a fate similar to his had befallen his nephew, despite all his efforts to prevent it. My mother though couldn't contain herself, nor could my father manage to calm her down. She kept beating her chest and crying out aloud, cursing the Goddess for destroying her family. She began to abuse the Goddess like she would any woman who had stolen her son from her.

I haven't shared something until now because it is so embarrassing, but such was her agony that she even wet herself as she wailed inconsolably.

As I followed the family from the river where I bathed to the temple, sporting the saree, I didn't know whether to celebrate my triumph or to mourn their loss, a loss they would never come to accept. Their pain began to weigh me down as I walked behind them in what felt like the longest walk ever.

The second part of the initiation is performed by Jogathis, where the senior-most welcomes the new entrant into the Jogathi fold. This is a grand affair, almost like a mini-wedding. It signifies the discarding of all markers of the identity held until then and of taking on a whole new personality, a new name, a new life and becoming a member of a whole new community. Looking back, especially now that I am a mother to so many, something churns within as I imagine the pain my parents must have felt at that time. How can I blame them for how they treated me? I remember that during the rituals in the temple, my only prayer was that the Goddess would grant my parents the strength to bear the pain they were experiencing. 'As You accept me as Your own from this day, bless those who have given me birth and raised me to this day, where they submit me to You,' I prayed as tears kept rolling down my face.

Like all traditions, the rituals have evolved and changed over a period of time. We now invite all the girls in the neighbourhood to participate. We make the initiate sit on a wooden seat and perform a turmeric-applying ceremony like they do for brides, cut the old thread and tie a ritual thread, do aarti and announce to all that she now belongs to our community. Then we gift her a new padligi, with a new deity made especially for her, as well as beads.

We gently place a lit neem stem on the tongue as a purification ritual to nullify the effects of any ill words uttered or any bad deeds performed until then. This helps get rid of inhibitions and simply gives Jogathis a new lease of life. A mantra is then whispered into her ear that is to be her only code of conduct for the rest of her life. 'Feed the hungry, call those who you see in the sun to the shade, and if anyone were to talk of footwear or whistle when you eat, or if there is a death in the village, then no food is to be had there until the funeral procession leaves the village, because it is inauspicious for those who bear the Goddess within and on their heads,' was whispered into my ear. Jogathis are not allowed to eat in a village where there has been a death. If the mortal remains are kept overnight, we eat in the neighbouring village. As we administer this oath, we also ask initiates to ensure it is followed until death.

At the end of it all, it comes as a huge relief to have a community to call your own. The ceremony easing us into our new identity is like a homecoming. These rituals marked the beginning of my journey of motherhood, and enabled me to embrace not just other Jogathis but people from across the world, regular people like you.

My greatest joy is to see those who have left their homes and come to me, accepting me as their mother, be welcomed by their parents and families after knowing that they have joined us as part of our performing art troupe. Such is the power of this cultural inheritance. Such is its potential to transform lives, like it has mine, that I wish we could do more to ensure its pursuit, much more than what I have been able to so far.

4

When Death Beckoned

It is one thing to desire change and quite another to live through it. Today, I stand tall like a banyan tree with my roots in the form of my art, my disciples and the respect I have earned. But there was a time when I felt like a plant in the sea that no one takes refuge under; nor does it bear fruit of any worth.

That's how I was made to feel when I went home after the initiation. All was well for two to three days, after which the effect of my transformation began to strike everyone. Yet again, I was at the receiving end of their unease and angst. Maybe they didn't know what to make of me. Or maybe it was too much for my parents to actually see their son as a woman.

If I sat inside the house they would ask why I was at home, if I ventured out they would ask why I was going around town. If I went to fetch water, I would be admonished for talking to the girls but neither was I allowed to talk to the boys. If I wasn't to be seen anywhere, what was I to do, where was I to go? Anything I did or said invited the wrath of my father who would want to beat me at times, but would restrain himself since I carried the Goddess within me.

Two weeks passed by and my father eventually began to avoid being in the same space as me. He wanted me to sit in a corner and not engage with anyone while I longed to be with people. 'Get lost!' he would often yell. By the end of the third week my disappointment and despair got the better of me. If my being alive was the sole reason for the pain and suffering of those around me, then let me end the cause, I thought. I couldn't stand the pitiful looks I got from some people; others would loudly, in my presence, bemoan the fate that had befallen the Setty family. 'After all, the Goddess spares no one if she decides to possess someone,' they'd say. This prompted me to go to Davanagere and buy a bottle of pesticide; I consoled myself saying it would all come to an end very soon.

On my way back from Davanagere, I stopped at a home to which I had been invited so that the family could pay their respects to me for having been initiated. It is customary to invite and worship new Jogathis and to fill their caskets with offerings such as rice, jowar, vegetables and so on. They serve sweets on a plantain leaf and place it in front of us to worship us for being a vehicle of the Goddess. Of course, these days you see much less of such devotion because fewer people take to this way of life due to the strict regimen it calls for.

I left that house that evening and was walking on a bridge across a canal when I stopped, looked this way and that and saw there was no one around. I placed the deity I was carrying on the side of the road and pulled out the bottle of pesticide from inside my blouse. I wrestled to open the bottle. All I wanted to do was bring the saga to an end. But the bottle refused to open. I cracked the bottle open by knocking it on the edge of the road and in one gulp, swallowed the entire potion. Then I pulled out a piece of jaggery from the casket and shoved it into my mouth, chewing hard to disguise the taste of 'death'. As the jaggery melted into sweetness I hurried home, only to be greeted by a furious father. He asked me where I had been all this while, and as I gave him details, my mother asked me to have my dinner. I told her I had eaten and, as instructed by my father, went inside to sleep.

To this day, if I get a whiff of petrol or kerosene, it recalls the memory of my tryst with death. I relive the entire experience, even almost four decades on, and feel like throwing up as the trauma of that time returns as a flashback.

At the time, though, I was worried my family members might smell the pesticide. By then the poison had begun to curdle my insides and I slept holding my knees close to my chest with my arms wrapped around them. I was foaming at the mouth, my head was spinning and in the intensity of all that was happening I seemed to have slipped into a state of unawareness. I threw up.

My father woke up at around 4 a.m. and, upon seeing my state, woke me up, told me to clean up and go back to sleep. He dismissed it as a case of indigestion; my mother gave me a cloth to wipe my mouth and clean up. I went out to throw the cloth but couldn't muster the courage to come back in, so I slept on the verandah. And that's all the memory I have of that night. I gained consciousness only after two weeks in hospital.

It appears that my mother, seeing me asleep past sunrise, tried to wake me up. She came near to sprinkle water on me and smelt the pesticide. All hell broke loose as she wailed loudly and ran towards my father's factory. My father is said to have rushed home and taken me to the hospital in Davanagere. Doctors refused to admit me and so my father took me to the Chigateri General Hospital. Although I was semi-conscious through it all, I have no memory of the two weeks that followed as I recovered.

But when I finally was back on my feet after two weeks, there was no one from home around. They had left when the doctor refused to discharge me at the end of two weeks saying it was a police case and, besides, I would have to stay back in the hospital to recover from the trauma. The hospital authorities suggested they all go home and come back later, but neither did they return, nor did I hear from anyone as I spent the next two weeks recovering. However, the hospital not only gave me a second lease of life, it also marked the beginning of my dance of destiny. It is here that I started dancing to entertain fellow patients and staff. With the thambige vessel on my head I would dance, much to the amusement of the nurses and other patients who were very warm towards me. Some inmates and visitors, even hospital staff, would reward me with coins and at the end of two weeks, I had collected a good ten to twelve rupees!

It was here that I met the first set of people who accepted me as I am and gave me love and strength to face the challenges of this world. Manju in the bed next to mine was suffering from brain fever. His mother and uncle, on knowing that no one from my home had returned to see me, began to treat me as their own son. From food to medicines, they took care of everything I needed. All the loaves of bread that the hospital provided would be stacked aside since they brought me fresh home-made food every day. I didn't know anything about them, nor can I remember where they came from, but it was their kindness that helped me survive those two weeks.

The administrative staff had me discharge myself and, eyes welling up with tears because none of my family was there and I felt orphaned, I packed up all the dry loaves of bread collected over my time there, the cash I had 'earned', and left for Kukwada. When I reached home, it sunk in that I was indeed orphaned. It was quite late and I was already anxious as to what my parents would say. But they said nothing, nor did any of my siblings. There was a strange, mournful silence. I didn't have the courage to ask why they hadn't come to the hospital or why I was being meted this silent treatment. I went to the kitchen to check if there was any leftover food and found there was only some saaru (a lentil soup, like rasam) left. I took out the loaves of dry bread, dipped them in the saaru and ate, then went to bed, feeling abandoned within my own home. I laid my head in the lap of an eerie silence as my ceaseless stream of thoughts sang a raucous lullaby. I was better off at the hospital, I thought, and wondered why I had come back home.

The morning was no better as the silent treatment continued. When I went to sweep the house, my sister took the broom away from me. I tried to clean the threshold; my other sister took away the bowl of red soil that we used to decorate it with. I was being told in no uncertain terms that I no longer belonged in my home. Nobody said anything but it was as if they were pushing me to the point where I would walk out on my own. So, I just finished my morning rituals and left to visit some homes in the village that day and returned only around sunset to do my evening pooja.

My father had gone to Davanagere and got a saree and blouse to conduct the pooja done after five weeks of being a Jogathi. This ritual also involves cooking food from the grains gathered over those five weeks of seeking alms, inviting five Jogathis over, filling the padligi and so on. The thought that my family was willing to perform this ritual was some consolation.

The house was now echoing the silent discomfort around my presence. I went to my neighbours and as I started talking, it was as if the barrage that had held all the thoughts and discussions in and around my house during those two weeks and upon my return broke open. 'How many parents would willingly get their son initiated onto the Jogathi order? Don't Jogathis manage to make a life and a living? What was the need for you to drink poison and try to kill yourself?' they asked. I had no answers and sat there listening to all of them with moist eyes and a guilt-ridden heart.

There was a Haalaswamy Matha just opposite our house where villagers would gather for bhajans every evening. It was normally a loud affair, but on that day it sounded haunting, and even the lyrics of the bhajans began to feel like they were aimed at me or were reflections on my life. I kept time with the cymbals half-heartedly as thoughts about my despicable state began to overcome me. '*Yaarige Yarilla ... yeravina samsaara ... neerina megala gulle nijavalla hariye,*' they sang and I began to wonder at the depth of the meaning of those words. Does no one belong to anyone? Is life but a bubble on the surface of water? Is this the way life is?

Just then, my father went over to Narasimhamurthy, the head of the team that led the bhajan every evening, and told him he had something to discuss. My heart sank as I overheard their conversation. 'No parent will agree to do it, but we have. We spent money and arranged for the ritual and on our own have ensured he gets what he wished for and let him be a Jogathi. But even then, he went and drank poison and brought shame upon us yet again,' my father said. 'Also, if he had been a girl, we would have got her married and sent off to her husband's house, and if he was a boy, we would have found a match and had him settle down. But he is neither. If he had been blind or physically challenged, we would have kept him home and fed him for the rest of our lives. But he fits nowhere and has become a Jogathi so let him go and live the way Jogathis do. Let him not be in front of our eyes. Whatever he has collected all these days has been kept intact. Also, tomorrow is Friday, and we also have to do the ritual of the first month anniversary, which we will. But henceforth, let him not hover around here,' he said, in a tone of finality.

'What do you have to say, Manju?' asked Narasimhamurthy. What could I say? Or rather what was left to say when the one who brought you into this world had distanced himself from you and asked you to fend for yourself? The turmoil stirred up by those words was almost like the one I had experienced when I was in the lap of death as the poison had begun to eat me from within. Tears kept rolling down my cheeks, but I didn't say much except agree with what they were saying.

I overheard Narasimhamurthy ask my father, 'But where will he go? What will he do in the world outside? It is difficult to imagine, but if that's what you have decided, we pray and hope that the Goddess who brought him to this state will also take care of him in the future.'

That was all the hope I had too. That the one who had shown me Her presence wouldn't abandon me like all the others had. Today, as I look back on all that I have faced as well as achieved, I know She has. Recently, there was a television show in which little children replayed my life story. I was all tears reliving those memories. Kannada superstar actor and director Ravi Chandran said the same thing—that if I hadn't been forced to leave home, I would probably not be standing here today as an icon, a role model and an inspiration for countless people across the globe.

Back then, when the day to leave finally arrived, I realized I wasn't prepared for it. Never had I dreamt that I would be asked to leave the home and the people I called my own. But then that's life, the cruellest master one can imagine. I could see my mother struggling to accept my father's diktat, but there wasn't much she could do either. She prepared for the ritual with a heavy heart and moist eyes. I could sense her pain and anxiety but I was helpless.

A seat was laid, the saree was dutifully wrapped, food was served, which I struggled to swallow. The sweet dish too tasted as bitter as the poison and I left it half-eaten. For the first time ever, I didn't hear my mother admonish me for not eating well, for getting up without finishing my meal; for the first time she didn't advise me on how important it was for children to eat to their heart's content. I guess she knew how difficult it was for me to gulp down the morsels knowing they were my last at home. It felt like a house in mourning.

Tears wet my chest as I picked up my meagre belongings and headed to the bus stand. No goodbyes were said, no words spoken. The farewell felt more like a funeral where this physical form was being distanced by those who no longer wished to have it around. Although my father walked with me to the bus stand, he uttered not a word, nor did he ask me where I was going. I stood watching as he turned back to return home.

It was 1985 and I was all of twenty-one years old, alone, distraught and lost. I had nowhere to go, nothing to be, no one to call my own but myself and my choice to live life the way I wished to. As fancy as that last line sounds, it was anything but that. It was death in a new avatar. A death that was pushing me to find life anew for it had already shown me how difficult it was to really die.

I made straight for Radhamma's house. She had been a tower of strength during my hospital stay and so I shared with her my latest ordeal. I spent two days at her place, trying to recover from all that had happened. That Tuesday, Radhamma took me to a temple nearby where an old woman lived close by and worshipped the deity Huchangiyellamma. I started helping her with temple chores, cleaning the pooja vessels, wiping the floor clean and the like; she gave me a place to live and shared the food that people in her house gave her. Initially accommodating and nice to me, eventually she began to abuse me. Radhamma then advised me to rent a place for myself and live independently.

'Anyway you go seek alms and sing and pray and earn the grains and basic money you require. Why then should you be an uninvited guest?' she said. I saw sense in her words. She found me a place in Jalinagara of Davanagere district where her sister lived. The rent was fifty rupees. She also gave me an old stove, some utensils, a mattress, some sheets and a pillow, and this marked the beginning of my independent life. Alone, armed only with my padligi with which to sustain myself, I started my new life in a new little town.

I would go to Kukwada every Tuesday and Friday since that was the only other place I knew; I would earn some rice that I would exchange at a store for money. I would then ask the storekeeper to keep the money safe and collect it once a month when it was time to pay the rent. On weekends, I would make an additional eight to ten rupees. This way, I managed to pay the rent and save some money for myself.

At first, the trips to Kukwada were difficult because I would meet people who had known me since childhood; often, they would have some 'great advice' to offer: for instance, had you continued with your studies, you would have easily landed a government job. Others would stand around gossiping loud enough for me to hear, saying look what the Goddess reduced his life to, she spares no one, how sad … I slowly began to ignore what fell on my ears because there was nothing I could do brooding over these comments. It had been my choice to be a woman and if this is what it came with, so be it, I thought and carried on.

But the travails of being a woman are many, I realized, with each passing day. One incident that took place within the first few days of trying to be independent scared and scarred me to such an extent that to this day, the memories send a shiver down my spine. This is one incident I wish had never taken place. It was the second time that I wanted to end my life.

What happened was this: One evening, I was returning home with money collected from selling the rice I had gathered over the month. I had to pay the house rent for two months and I was behind with the payment. I boarded the bus and headed home. Upon alighting, I took the shorter route home. It was a deserted stretch, barely lit. Today, it looks completely different with street lights and large buildings around. But back then it was a nook for drunkards. As I crossed the high school field, four men who were sitting and drinking in a corner stopped me and asked how much money I had. 'Shell it out,' they said. I could feel my calf muscles go weak but I didn't show my fear. I tried to evade them saying, 'From where would I have any money, anna.' That only rubbed them the wrong way and in their intoxication they unleashed the beasts within themselves on me.

I dread to relive those moments. They tore off my blouse, snatched the bundle of rice I was carrying and threw it away. Both my honour and all my earnings in the form of rice grains lay scattered on the floor. The night sky was witness to this mute wail of helplessness as they ripped off my saree, even as I pleaded with them to be spared. I tried to escape their clutches and run, but as soon as I went a few steps, they caught hold of me and threw me to the ground. They had lost all sense of being human and took turns to ravage my body and my being. I thought this was the end, they would kill me. I held their feet and cried aloud for mercy but all those screams only fuelled their evil masculinity, which they were flaunting by tearing my dignity apart.

Once their demonic selves felt contented or maybe they were exhausted, they walked away with all the money I had. I lay there wailing loudly but the vastness of the ground and the darkness of the night swallowed everything into its killing silence. What was the meaning of such a life, which was a living hell? What did I do to deserve one devastating punishment after another? I picked up the bits of my existence that lay discarded all around and painfully walked home.

As I reached home, the vastness of that tiny room once again pierced my heart. There was no one with whom to share, no one to care if I was alive or dead, no one I could cry my heart out to and lament over my fate's cruel twists. I cried alone. The walls of that tiny room watched my thoughts crumble my will to live. Was death calling again, I wondered. But my recent failed attempt at dying had already made me realize that it looked all too easy to try to die. However, death isn't simple. To this day, I shudder at the thought of that night. Every time I read about incidents of rape or molestation and injustice against women, I shiver. Physically, I was a man, right? If those monsters could treat a male body this way, it angered and frightened me to wonder what they could do a female body.

Surviving death made me realize that trying to escape the ordeal called life was not a fool-proof solution. Or to put it simply, it wasn't easy to die. And God forbid, should you not die successfully, you invite pain and trouble that are worse than whatever you tried to escape. Maybe this time I could use some other route to death, I thought, and wondered if lying on the rail track would do it. Just at that moment, I felt a strange thirst and got up and had a large jug of water. By the time I gulped down the last mouthful, I had discarded the idea of dying. Why should I die? For what fault of mine should I give up my life?

If this is what life had thrown at me, so be it. I would prove that I was way stronger. I looked at the Goddess and told her to punish those who had done this to the one who had chosen to walk Her path. That reminder that She was within me gave me strength and I told myself this was all a part of life and I needed to keep going. Fear could kill, doubt could kill. And I had to kill both these before they killed me. I wiped my tears and went to bed with the hope of a better morning.

And it was indeed a better morning. I went and told the house owner all that had happened. He not only gave me strength but also told me I didn't need to pay him rent for two months. His generosity gave me strength and made me believe in the goodness of people.

It provided a breather. Although I saved and paid him after two months, at that time his words were a great support.

Since that day, whenever I meet youngsters or students who ask me how to overcome difficulties, I tell them to go drink a large jug of water if they feel under tremendous pressure. Because it is just about breaking the train of thought for that one vulnerable moment. Gulping down a large jug of water breaks that chain for more than a few moments and soothes jittery nerves.

That was also the last time I ever thought of dying. Although I wish those events had not taken place, I feel that they probably also strengthened my resolve to fight and fuelled my determination to survive.

5

Jogathi Nritya—My Art, My Lifeline

Life teaches us that change is constant. By the time you arrive at some conclusions about it, you are put through experiences that render them irrelevant. As I left home, I thought I was relegating my dreams of singing and dancing to history. It was all about survival now. And without a family, a house or even a village or town to call my own, what could I dream of?

When I was struggling as Manju, I used to enjoy my solitude. Since it spared me the horror of ceaseless taunts, I used to feel great joy when people left me alone. It let me wander into the land of dreams and fancies. But reality struck too soon, and now this solitude was anything but enjoyable. I had to be my own hero and my own family because there was no one else who would put food on my plate. So, keeping all else aside, I focussed on earning a few rupees. Dutifully, I would go every Tuesday and Friday to the village and to fairs on weekends to earn as much as I could by way of rice, vegetables, chillies and money. With the money I would buy oil, jaggery, tea dust, soap and save some to pay the rent. I had begun to make peace with this meaningless existence, occasionally berating myself for having brought it upon myself.

But before I could submit to a life of doom and despair, life shone tiny rays of sunshine upon me in the form of Appaji or Father. He gave me the magic wand of Jogathi nritya, which turned my life around. Kalavva taught me to use that wand and the village of Chilakanahatti stood behind me and helped me cast the magic spell that made me who I am today. To a person who had been disowned by her father and mother and cast out of her village, life handed a new set of all these. In retrospect, I can vouch for the truth that nature leaves no place vacant and no need unfulfilled.

I met Appaji by chance. His name was Matikallu Basappa, I called him Appaji. One day, I was seeking alms at a bus stand in Davanagere when I saw a large crowd and heard the sound of the chaudaki, a folk musical instrument, from a distance. I also headed there thinking that if nothing else, I could earn a few extra rupees. When I went closer, I saw an old man dressed in a lungi and shirt, holding the taala (cymbals) in his left hand and playing the chaudaki shruthi instrument with his right as he sang along, while a very young boy, sporting a long braid, danced to the music. I stood and watched them perform three–four songs and spared them a few coins from my day's collection.

Back then, people had to wait for a long time for the bus. I saw that when a sizeable number of people had gathered, the man would begin to perform. When the bus arrived and they all left, he would smoke a beedi, chew some paan and sit back and wait for the next lot of people. I watched while about four batches of people gathered and departed. I was besotted by the boy's dancing and my feet naturally took me to them. 'Appaji!' I called out and asked if he would teach me to dance like the boy. We then got talking. He asked me about myself and I recounted the story of my life so far. He heard me out and agreed to teach me; he invited me to his home.

'You can watch your tamma (younger brother) and learn,' he said. The boy, Parashurama, was his son and had become a Jogathi at that young age. He was dancing with the Goddess, carrying a pot on his head. I accompanied the father–son duo to their house that evening, had dinner with them and returned home.

That was a night my dreams were rekindled, literally. In all my excitement to learn dance, I just couldn't go to bed. So I placed a small pot on my head and kept moving around in my tiny house, trying some moves and patting my back, feeling good about it. Finally, when fatigue got the better of me, I went to sleep only to dream of dancing with people in the market. The sound of claps and whistles was so loud that I woke up with a jerk. I was glad to be dreaming again, both literally and metaphorically. I went back to sleep, eagerly awaiting an early dawn.

The next day I reached Appaji's house and began what was to be almost a year-long apprenticeship, an unpaid one at that. He first made me practise by balancing an ordinary pot on my head while I did some moves. In the market I would sit and watch Parashurama dance and mentally make notes of all the moves and steps. It took me three or four months to learn all the steps and get the moves right. Nothing fancy, just simple steps, not like the attractive moves dancers use these days. But my deep desire to learn didn't let me sleep until I had mastered the art. Once I had learned well, Appaji started taking me with him to perform on Fridays and Sundays. I imbibed many life lessons touring with him this way. I didn't earn a single pie, though. I danced for hours together at times, yet he wouldn't pay me a single rupee nor give me some time to rest. We didn't speak much either.

I remember we went once to the chilli fair at Ranibennur. Those days farmers who came to such fairs were also very devoted. They honoured Jogathis wholeheartedly and paid them handsomely in kind. This fair earned Appaji four large sacks of chillies but, as was the norm, I didn't get even a handful. I wonder what made him act that way.

We went around the village all day, dancing in front of every single house. As dusk fell we headed towards the fields where those working there formed groups and asked for Yellamma's story to be narrated. Appaji would sing and I would dance gleefully. As the spectators applauded and whistled I would dance with greater zeal, adding many more attractive moves and gestures. It was physically draining but nothing fuels an artist more than the sound of cheering. I would be dead as we headed back home. And he would be flush with the produce the farmers would generously offer as a token of appreciation for having told the tale of the Goddess and entertained them.

It went on this way for almost a year, after which I slowly distanced myself from the duo and joined another team of Jogathis, Girijamma and Bhagamma, who were much respected in and around Davanagere.

A few years ago, I met Parashurama at a temple fair and was saddened to see him looking frail and loitering all by himself. He came up to me and said that Basappa had passed away a few years ago and he now lived alone. I gave him some money and we parted. I haven't heard from him since. But till my last breath I shall remember both of them with a lot of reverence and respect, because even though they didn't give me a single rupee, they gave me the art which today has earned me all that I have, which helped win love, respect and recognition for the entire community. Maybe the year-long unpaid internship was the fee for acquiring this art. This art has not only kept me alive, it has transformed me from just another transgender seeking alms on the street to an internationally recognized folk artist.

Most important, Appaji became a father figure to the bruised, orphaned heart of a twenty-year-old and helped it heal and find a new lease of life.

Soon after I joined Girijamma and Bhagamma, it was time for the Huligi temple fair and I got busy with the preparations for it. I had to save up for the bus fare, which was thirty-five rupees, and to buy a few sarees at the fair. Old sarees would be sold and new ones bought.

When I arrived in Huligi, I was overwhelmed by a storm of memories. Exactly a year ago my entire family, even if with a heavy heart, had accompanied me to this temple for the initiation. A year later, here I was, all alone, abandoned. Tearfully I made my way into the temple town which became my home for the next forty-five days. I managed to pick up two new sarees at the fair, one for three rupees and the other for two.

As I have said before, each time I have been beset by intense pain, the Goddess has always shown me a way out. It was no different this time. While I had felt homeless when I reached, after I left I landed in a village that came to be my refuge, my solace and practically the sculptor of my now distinguished destiny. After Basappa, it is the people of Chilakanahatti village whom I bow down to in gratitude for supporting me and shaping me into an artist of some standing.

At the fair I met a distant paternal relative who invited me to Chilakanahatti, where he lived with his wife and ran a hotel. I could not say no to him, so to avoid that I said I would come along only if he promised to get me a saree. I didn't expect him to, but he agreed and said that he would not just get me a saree but also conduct the rituals that customarily honour those who 'carry' the Devi. After this, I had no choice but to go along with him

I went to Chilakanahatti, intending to stay there for a week; I stayed back for a month. But since there was no mention of the saree, nor did it look like he had mentioned it to his wife, who was a headstrong woman, I decided to go about my usual rounds. I got the bhajan singers of the village to join me and we would go around singing and seeking alms. On some days I would go around alone.

Everyone welcomed me with warmth; the villagers accepted me as one of their own. The people in every house I visited would generously give me alms and fill my padligi with grains, rice and good vegetables. They called me 'Setru Jogamma' and treat me with a lot of respect. It felt strangely satisfying to be addressed this way because until then I had only been rebuked and abused for bringing dishonour to the family name. The villagers themselves advised me not to go around with the bhajan singers but to pick up a chowdaki, as is the Jogathi tradition, and sing along. When I admitted to not knowing how to play it, they arranged to introduce me to Somakka of Golarahalli, with whom I could team up.

Here was a village taking responsibility to settle a transgender nomad, a Jogathi who didn't even belong to their village, out of sheer goodness and respect for those who had been chosen by the Goddess.

That is how I met Somakka Jogathi who came looking for me in Chilakanahatti. I was apprehensive as she was quite senior to me and I was new to all this.

'Come, let me teach you a few songs,' she said, and made me recite after her. A few songs later, she gave her stamp of approval but added that I had much to learn. From there began our long association. She taught me many songs and we also performed Yellamma's story.

The first time I sang in front of a mic was at the temple. I was elated. The mic, tied to a wooden staff, was firmly planted in the soil. The reception that performance received was beyond imagination; people filled our caskets with wonderful things that day. That warmth and that appreciation is what a novice artist needs when he/she begins his/her journey, for it puts all other fears to rest. Those villagers were the perfect connoisseurs: they held my hand and boosted my spirits.

My bond with Somakka only grew stronger and we began to perform everywhere and earn well, both in cash and in kind. It felt good to have people call me Setru Jogamma and even specially spread a cloth for me to sit on when we went into the fields to perform. It is on one such occasion that Somakka informed Kalavva about me. I had been introduced to her earlier when Gandhi maava had met her around the time of my initiation. He had told her about me and requested her to take me under her wings and teach me to sing, carry the pot, dance, play the chowdaki and so on. But I was too scared to follow up, thanks to all the tales that surrounded her.

People said that she practised witchcraft, that she was always drunk and that she beat people when she was intoxicated. I had stayed away for fear of being 'captured' by this strange woman. People said she kept Jogathis captive and took away all their earnings. But life had other plans—fortunately.

One day, Kalavva landed up at Chilakanahatti along with Somakka and Bannikal Ramavva. 'You are Gandhi's nephew, right?' she asked, to which I meekly nodded. 'C'mon, sing!' she said. I shook my head to say no. Then she sang a song to which I danced, much to her approval. That day they all went to seek alms in Haaruvanahalli and returned to my house at night. I had cooked dinner for all of them. Once again Kalavva expressed her appreciation and said that I cooked better than many girls. It felt like an award.

This was when she initiated me into theatre. I had never done a play before and I told her that I would rather sit and watch. 'Does everyone come with experience?' she asked. 'How can you know until you learn? One learns as one does things and you too shall,' she said, and asked me to get my make-up done and dance when she told me to.

I did not know how to get my face painted. Basalingamma Jogathi applied make-up and I watched my face transform. It was a unique experience, all new to me—the stage, the act, the audience, the preparations, the magic that constituted putting up a play.

I sat and watched like an awestruck child as the other team members played their parts, said their lines, moved to Kalavva's instructions. Kalavva's call would break this reverie and I would stumble in my hurry to dance. All my apprehensions seemed to vanish into thin air when I would see the audience in front of me, hear the sound of the whistles and claps each time I swayed, drowning out the voices of fear in my head.

Those were days when people came to watch not just as spectators but as devotees, and so every time there was a scene in which, say, a character had to be presented with gifts, like Renuka Devi when she had her baby shower, or the mendicant soothsayer Koravanji who came seeking alms, members of the audience would actually offer grains and fruits and so on. It was organic interactive theatre. They were all part of the play and that made it so much more beautiful. It was almost like the unfolding of a chapter of our religious history in a different time and era. All that changed with the advent of television and modernization, and in this era of mobile phones we do not see the younger generation even hovering around such plays, and even if they do, they do not have the patience to sit through all of it.

The initiation into the world of folk theatre made me adore Kalavva and her ways of teaching and training new Jogathis. It dispelled all the fears I had previously had about her. It also strengthened my faith in the Goddess because even though I had tried hard to stay away from Kalavva, She had brought her to me and poured this wealth of art into my bosom.

With the help of the villagers I began to balance both the pursuit of this form of theatre as well as earning

my living. Kalavva would call me whenever there were
plays; I would go to participate in them and then return
to Chilakanahatti. The villagers stood by me when I
moved out of my relative's house and began to live on
my own.

For instance, the family of Sulekallu Veerupanna and
Susheelamma, to this day, even with the third generation
growing up, see me as one of their own. Our association
began when I used to sit outside their house to avoid
sitting where everyone else was waiting for the bus
because there were always boys who would make fun
of me, or say something nasty. His daughter had come
home for her baby's delivery and I used to play with and
take care of the infant. That is how I bonded with the
family.

One day, I had a tiff with the relatives in whose house
I lived. My uncle's wife was angry with me because I
had told her that her daughter was having an affair and
suggested she watch the girl's activities. For three days
after that, I didn't eat there. Nor could I eat anywhere
else because of caste equations. My head was spinning,
I could barely walk. In that state I happened to reach
Veerupanna's house. They were having a house-warming
ceremony. When they saw how pale I was, they asked if
something was wrong.

I used to address him and his wife as Kakka and
Kakki. I explained my situation to Kakki. First, she
admonished me for staying hungry. As she then sat me
down to lunch, she said something that I don't think

even the most educated and liberal persons to this day will have the heart to say. 'Look, dear one,' she said. 'You call me Kakki, so I couldn't care less what caste you belong to. I have four boys and one daughter. You can count yourself either as one of my five sons or one of my two daughters. But from today, never will you go hungry. Stay here. Even if I have just one roti, we will both share a half each, don't worry.'

I broke down. How could one be grateful enough for such love and unconditional acceptance, I wondered. The male physical form and the female being within were both finding acceptance. 'If your body is that of a man, we will take you as a son and if your heart is of a woman, be our daughter.' That is what they said to me. Their love for and acceptance of me is forever etched in my heart. It was this acceptance and love that I had been seeking; finding that was liberating. To this day, this family is closest to my heart. One of their grandsons recently had a house-warming ceremony and he sent me a saree when he bought clothes for the rest of the family. This kind of acceptance can achieve a change that no legislation can.

A man called Gurulingappa who worked as a forest guard offered me a room at his house and said I could tutor his children in the evenings. I also learnt tailoring from his wife during my brief stay with them until they got transferred. Just when I wondered what life would throw my way now, the villagers advised me to settle into a rented house; they helped me find one and provided all the basic things I would require to live there.

It was not always possible to manage with what I earned from singing and seeking alms. One of the villagers suggested I start making and selling idlis in the morning. I took up this suggestion and started selling idlis from home, but since I lived at one end of the village, they didn't find many takers. Before I could get disheartened, the villagers suggested I take the idlis around the village to sell. This worked. By 7.30 a.m. all the idlis would be sold out. I would make two kilos of idlis and chutney to go with them each day and sell four idlis for one rupee. Until I got busy with plays for Kalavva, I sold idlis every single day, without fail, for eight to nine months.

This is why the thought of paying 218 rupees for three idlis and one vada at Bengaluru airport stunned me. This was way beyond my imagination, I guess!

Chilakanahatti, in a way, gave me everything: Appaji, Avva, a new home, an art, a means of earning and leading an independent, respectable life. Everything that I had lost since I left home was mine again. It reinstated my faith in myself and pushed me to work harder. Evenings would be spent teaching children. It felt good that although my body had not cooperated when I was in school and wanted to study, I was able to facilitate learning for so many whose futures would be brighter. And the most fairytale-like testimony to the honest efforts made back then is a recent incident that left not just me but an entire village audience speechless.

In April 2022, I was invited to a programme in Kudligi. A soldier called Katera Ramesh had retired from service and was returning to the village and some people were organizing a welcome march for him along with other serving soldiers and army veterans from the region. They wanted me to inaugurate that function. I had not been feeling well but when I told them so, they insisted I come anyway. They said they would take me to the doctor if necessary but they wanted me in Kudligi, even if only for the inaugural. 'It is fine if you do not address the gathering,' they said, but insisted that they wished to felicitate me.

The next day, I went to the pharmacist and bought some general medicine since the doctor was unavailable at the hospital. I took all of it and went to Kudligi. As I got down from the car, the villagers thronged me for a selfie. I was too exhausted even to smile for so many of them, but had to oblige. At that point the soldier whose open jeep had just reached offered his respects by doing namaskar to me. I blessed him from where I was but by the time I could turn around he had alighted and come down to my car. Even before I could take a look at his face, he bowed down, touched my feet and embraced me. I was taken aback. I didn't even know him and the sudden hug threw me off. I clearly looked perplexed but what followed was even more shocking.

'Amma, your words and letters are in my heart, and your blessings are on me,' he said. What was this man saying? I asked him what he meant. That's when he explained, saying, 'Amma I was among the boys who used to take tuition from you in Chilakanahatti, which was my grandparents' place. You taught me to write and read as a child, Amma. Your blessings are what have made me worth all this today, Amma.'

I had goosebumps and my hands began to tremble from the sheer intensity of those words. I thanked the organizers in my mind for enabling this meeting and this surreal experience. Just as I was absorbing all the warmth from this exchange, the soldier's wife also came around and said, 'Amma, I too studied under your guidance. I am from Chilakanahatti.' Then she gave me details of her family.

The warmth of this reunion left me teary-eyed for days, and made me feel grateful once again to all those people, especially in Chilakanahatti, who had stood by me back then.

Manjamma outside her old house

Posing with the traditional Yellamma Koda (Yellamma's Pot) on her head

In the role of Keechaka in a play titled *Shivarjuna Yuddha*

In the role of a Lambani woman in a play on Yellamma titled *Renuka Devi Charitre*

Manjamma and
her troupe during
the Hampi Utsav
performance
in 2017

Bridal rituals for the new
initiate Jogathi

(Left and right) The Jogathi nritya dance

Jogathi nritya on the streets

Jogathi rituals—the new initiate being made to bear the padligi after the tying of the beads (mutthu kattisikollodu)

Manjamma (top row, centre) with her troupe at Hampi

Manjamma dressed for a play

Manjamma (left) during a dance practice session

Manjunath with his mother, B. Jayalakshmi

Manjamma in front of her old mud hut

Manjamma in her younger days

Manjamma weaving plastic bags

Manjamma's guru, Kalavva

(Left to right) Ramakka, Guru Kalavva and Manjamma

Guru Kalavva at the mic with Manjamma dancing on stage

Manjamma perfoming the writing-on-tongue ritual for the new initiate Jogathi

Manjamma perfroming the Jogathi nritya

Manjamma (left) teaching the Jogathi Nritya to fellow Jogathis

Manjamma in a white saree playing Renuka Yellamma

Manjamma as a shaman, administering traditional folk medicine to a patient

Performing Jogathi nritya at a temple fair

The Jogathis performing with the chowdaki and shruthi in their hands

Manjamma receiving the Karnataka Rajyotsava Award from then Chief Minister B.S. Yediyurappa

Being honoured by Hon. Governor of Karnataka Thawar Chand Gehlot

With Prime Minister Narendra Modi

Receiving the Padma Shri from then President Ram Nath Kovind

माता बी. मंजम्मा जोगती

मैं, भारत का राष्ट्रपति,
राम नाथ कोविन्द, व्यक्तिगत
गुणों के लिए आपके सम्मानार्थ,
पद्म श्री प्रदान करता हूँ।

नई दिल्ली
दिनांक 9 नवम्बर, 2021

राम नाथ कोविन्द
राष्ट्रपति

6

Ties and Threads

The love and acceptance I found in Chilakanahatti and the new world that my dance and theatre performances carved out for me in the tiny hamlets around were therapeutic and helped me forget the pain of abandonment. At the same time, the respect that this earned me brought all the scars back into my life.

In Chilakanahatti I realized I had three mothers—my biological mother, Gandhi maava who became my mother by virtue of having cut my waist thread, and my guru Kalavva. Each had nurtured me in their own way and made me who I am today.

While I was busy with my idlis, tuition and plays, Gandhi maava visited me. In fact, he had been the one who'd wanted me to train under Kalavva Jogathi and tried to have her take me as her apprentice right after I got initiated. But I had not gone that way then. Now that I was leading a respectable life and touring villages doing plays with her, he was happy. He came and took me back to Kampli for a few days. I was nervous, fearing a repeat of my last stint at his house, thrashings and all. But this time he showed a completely different side. Not only did he treat me well, he bought me things I needed for my house, and gifted me a saree when I left for Chilakanahatti two weeks later.

That was when I also forgave him for all that he had put me through. Maybe he was well-intentioned, I thought. He had not wanted me to go through what he had. I remembered that when I was a child, Gandhi maava had not been allowed to visit us. He longed to come and see his sister, my mother, but my father had forbidden it.

At the time, Gandhi maava was working at a factory in Harihara. My mother was the only sister he had wished to be in touch with. But since my father did not permit it and would abuse this 'woman-like creature', they would meet secretly by the bridge. I remember her stuffing rice and vegetables in a steel pot and pickle in a tumbler so no one would guess she was carrying food, and stealthily going to meet him. Upon her return, I would see her sitting in a corner, weeping. My father could not get a whiff of this, you see.

Still, she kept fighting with my father and reasoning with him for her brother to be allowed to come home. My mother was a fierce woman, not one to take anything lying down. When my father once had an affair with a much younger woman called Shivagangamma, my mother would fling vessels at him and fight fiercely, despite having to bear the brunt of his anger. About Gandhi maava, I remember her asking my father, 'How will the world accept him if I don't?' Eventually, my father relented; initially he gave permission for my uncle to visit only in my father's absence, later he made peace with him. Now, Gandhi maava told my parents that I had started life afresh and that I was doing well. This prompted my father to finally come and see me.

Interestingly, although my father wanted nothing to do with me after he threw me out of the house, he did give me one piece of advice. He said I should be careful not to bring him, our family and our community a bad name. This, I believe, has been the sole reason I did not go astray, did not disregard the sanctity of this identity, or let go of this art for a more lucrative way of living, like most other people. 'Do not be like others,' he'd said, as I picked up my meagre belongings and prepared to leave home that evening. 'These things do not happen in our caste, but you have chosen to be this way. Do not do anything that brings us a bad name. Do not bring a bad name to your own name, to us, to our caste. Wherever you live, live with respect.'

When he visited three years later, he seemed a little less upset than he was back then. He is said to have gone around Chilakanahatti enquiring about me and my ways of life. When he came to see me, he reiterated his expectation, albeit in a different tone. 'Look, my son, what has happened is your fate. Being a Jogamma is not something characteristic of our community, but lead a life of respect and keep our honour intact. That's all I ask of you,' he said. That visit paved the way for my mother and sisters to visit as well. I too went home, and even visited my brother in Kallukamba, the place that had once scared the living daylights out of me. My father finally accepted me as I was, but never as a daughter. He always addressed me as a son, till the end.

Still, not everything changed at once. For instance, when my brother got married a year later, I was not invited. They feared the bride's side would call off the wedding if they knew I had become a Jogathi, so they never even mentioned me to them. They had invited Gandhi maava and he had asked about me; by then he had developed a fondness for me.

'We have,' they said, 'but we aren't sure if he will turn up. The girl's folks aren't aware of him being a Jogathi.' The fact is that my brother had come to 'inform rather than invite' me. 'Look, I haven't spoken about you to my in-laws,' my brother said. 'It's up to you to attend the wedding or not.'

'You are basically asking me not to come, right?' I said.

'Yes,' he responded. 'No one in our community is going to give me a girl if they know you are this way. Which is why I have hidden it from them. Please don't come.' Then he left.

I began to brood over the bigotry of people. On the one hand, they wanted transgenders like us to come to functions to bless them and ward off evil; on the other, if we were part of their families, they did not want us to participate. If my own family saw me as inauspicious, what could I to expect from the world?

As if he had heard my thoughts, Gandhi maava came to Chilakanahatti and took me home to Kampli, thus preventing me from sinking again into the abyss of abandonment issues. He didn't want to leave me alone. Before leaving for the wedding he requested the neighbours to keep an eye so that I did not do anything to hurt myself. They took turns to keep me company.

At the wedding, though, someone apparently told the bride's family about me; they were saddened that my brother had kept this information from them since they were devotees of Yellamma. Devotion accomplished what kinship couldn't! 'Had she come, she would have blessed us all. Why did you have to hide this? Would we have called off the wedding when the Goddess Herself has chosen your son?' they asked my family. Reassured by the new relatives, my father came and took me to the Satyanarayana pooja conducted after the wedding. But such is the cycle of karma that in less than a decade, my brother came to me and said, 'Whichever girl you approve of, I shall marry her.'

Yes, it was a second marriage. Around 1998, we lost our father to blood cancer. After nearly a decade of marriage, my brother and his wife hadn't had a child and people had begun to talk. They said it was the Goddess's curse for not having invited me to the wedding. So, before he died, my father made my sister-in-law promise that she herself would preside over my brother's second marriage.

They did consider adoption, but the family couldn't agree on which child to adopt. My mother wanted a child from a relative on the paternal side, my sister-in-law was adamant about getting a child from her maternal family. My mother argued that that wouldn't be our bloodline. And so, with all this disagreement including the fact that my sister-in-law did not approve of a second marriage, what happened was that once when she was away at her parents' home, we fixed an alliance and my brother got married again.

Now, each time the two sisters-in-law fight with each other and complain about each other, I wonder why I arranged the second marriage. But back then, I was glad that I got to witness, bless and partake in my brother's wedding—so what if it was the second one. Within a year, my nephew was born, much to my mother's content and fulfilling my father's last wish, thus vindicating my choice and presence at the wedding.

Gandhi maava spent his final days at my place. He had an anal infection that left him writhing in pain. Once, when he was alone and could not take the suffering any longer, he sent word to my brother to come take him away. My brother took him to Kallukamba where my mother gave him room to sleep in the verandah outside in a shed-like space because the infection emitted an unbearable odour. Gandhi maava was inconsolable. 'Drop me at Manju's,' he kept muttering. Although I lived in a hut, I asked them to bring him over and that's how I got to tend to him during his last two months.

Taking care of him involved flushing out worms with medicine. The stench was unbearable. In fact, during those two months, none of the Jogathis would come inside the house. Even if they came by to help, they would cover their noses and struggle with the stench. Gandhi maava would scream and yell in pain; the only way to get him to sleep was liquor. Four packets of country liquor each day cost me twenty rupees, a huge amount back then; we did not always make that kind of money seeking alms. But I took care of him. I would lay him down outside and give him a bath, then put him back on the mat inside to sleep. The worms from his body would often crawl out onto the bed and up the wall.

Every morning, I would clean him up, wash his clothes and rewash everything with an antiseptic solution, take a bath and only then cook and eat. Everyone would ask how I tolerated the sight of those worms emerging endlessly, and endure the unbearable stench. When he passed away, I arranged for all the ceremonies because my other uncles, his brothers, refused to do so, saying he had become a Jogamma. He had spent a life of loneliness, owned nothing, saved nothing. Even the piece of land he had owned he sold for a dismal amount of money, and used it all up to eat, drink and live as he pleased.

He had been scared for me because of what his own life had been like. He was afraid that like himself, and many before him, I too would have to live uncared for, unwanted and finally unclaimed even as a dead body.

Perhaps this might have been so were it not for a lifeline called art and my guru, Kalavva.

Anyway, once back in Chilakanahatti after my brother's wedding, I got busy touring villages with Kalavva. I stopped selling idlis because I was on the move for most days in a month. Ours was the only team of Jogathis who performed the tale of Yellamma with such pomp. And it was Kalavva's wish or rather order that we prove that we were no less accomplished than others whose art had already been accorded respect or recognition.

Today, I see that I have paid the greatest respect I could to her dream of winning this art a respectable place in society and its artists the recognition they deserve. The art is what earned me my mother's love and acceptance. The mother who cursed Yellamma for having stolen her son from her, forgave Her, although with a heavy heart, when she saw that it was this very tradition that had made her son an artist. She was elated every time I received appreciation. Had she been around to see me receive the Padma Shri, I feel her heart would have stopped beating from joy. I too have had the joy of having two mothers with whom I shared an equally affectionate relationship. And both ensured I remain on good terms with the other.

Once when I had fought with my mother, I had stopped talking to her and even visiting home. Kalavva, upon hearing some people in Harapanahalli praise my performance exclaiming, 'Who is that blessed mother who gave birth to such a fine artist, he dances so well, sings so well,' asked me to go fetch my mother the following day so she could watch us perform. I refused. Kalavva threatened to throw me out of the play if I did not do as she said, and so I went home and asked for pardon. My mother first called me names and then gave me a kiss on the forehead. When I shared the reason for my visit, she readily agreed to come and watch the play.

Everyone there called me Parashurama even though I played four other roles in the play and danced between acts. My mother sat in the front row and heard people say, 'Parashurama's mother is here.' There is a scene depicting the interaction between Renuka Yellamma and Her son Parashurama. During this scene, my mother suddenly began to beat her chest and wail saying, 'You were my son but you became Her (Yellamma's) son. Is it for your sake that I gave birth to him?' Half the time, the audience was watching her respond to my performance.

I too wept profusely when I saw my mother cry. It recalled the time I was being initiated as a Jogathi; how much she had wept and cursed! Seeing me in a male role made her wish this was real and that her son had grown into a man as he now appeared on stage.

I thought she would be glad to see her son perform so well and that's what those consoling her also thought. But she said, 'No, no … my son would have been this way if my fate hadn't been this twisted. If his destiny hadn't been so dastardly, he would have grown up to be a man just like this. I wonder what was lacking in my worship! Had I not been cursed, my boy would look this way every day,' she wept.

Seeing her in so much pain was the most painful experience. Mothers have dreams for their children, different for sons and daughters. When a son is born, the aspirations are that he should look a certain way, he should be healthy and strong, he should always live like a king. A good education, a good bride, a house, some property ... these are the aspirations for a son so that he settles down. The dream for daughters is to bring them up gently, caringly, marry them into good families so that they have good family lives. These were typical rural dreams, say, five–six decades ago.

It tears me up to this day that my mother too would have nursed such dreams and that a boulder hit her gentle heart when I could be neither. She had delivered twenty-one children of whom only four had survived and I had turned out this way. It hurt me immensely to see her suffering.

But at least she had accepted me. Now that I had started doing plays, she felt proud that her son was making a name for himself. Although she didn't talk about how she felt, she would take drishti to ward off the evil eye whenever I got all dressed up. She would say, 'You know, I looked just like you, Manju, when I was young. Let me make sure my own eyes don't cast any ill on you.' Then she would kiss my forehead. If I complained lovingly that she was treating me like a child, she would respond, 'For me you will always be a child.'

Later, during the last four-five years of her life, she came to live with me in Gollarahalli, where I took care of her like she was a small child. I did everything a daughter would do, from taking her to the washroom, to scrubbing her back and giving her a bath, to taking care of her and dressing her up, and giving her a kiss after she was all dolled up. She ate a lot, taking tiny meals and snacks at regular intervals. I ensured I followed her food schedule to the T, even if it often went beyond my means. I would press her feet to help her sleep.

I would often lie with my head in her lap; she would talk to me. One day, she said, '*Manju, nannedurige neenu saibeku, kano* (Manju, you should die in front of my eyes, while I am alive).'

I was taken aback and asked why. 'Yes, I want you to go before me so that I can die in peace,' she said.

I still choke up when I remember that conversation. Stroking my head, she said, 'Yes, son. Your sisters have their husbands and children to take care of them. Your brother has two wives, and a son. All of my children except you has someone who will take care of them in their old age. Who do you have? Who will take care of you? If I die with this worry in my heart, I will be in great pain.' No mother wishes death for her child but mine did. Only a mother will feel such pain and worry.

When I began to get busy with programmes, she went to live with my younger sister for about five-six months after which she fell ill and was hospitalized. Once she recovered we brought her to my brother's place but her condition only worsened. This time the trip to the hospital was her last. After that, she lived either with me or my sisters. She passed away in 1995–96. Her absence haunts me even today, especially when I receive awards and honours.

With her passing, home is not the same, my sisters-in-law aren't as welcoming as she was. It is as if one thread has broken. The relationship is more a formality. So, even if I have programmes in Hospete where my brother lives, I stay at a hotel. If I have few hours before catching a train, I visit one of my daughters, my disciple Kavita, rest at her place and then head to the railway station.

However, I do visit relatives now. I keep in touch to show that despite them being distanced when I needed them the most, I am not disowning them now when I have respect and recognition. My siblings, too, began to accept me only after my younger brother succumbed to cancer. Grief brought them to accept me; the fear of losing yet another brother. But I have now put all of that behind me.

My Jogathi community will always come first. Just because I have been accepted by my biological family does not mean I will let them take the place of this community, which became family. I wish there was a way that enabled recognition of this mother-daughter bond too. Ours is a matrilineal community. I take fellow Jogathis as my sisters or daughters but there is no way I can legally acknowledge this bond. Although

I can't name them as my legal heirs and my nephew is my nominee with respect to documents, I have told my brother that after my death, no one from our family can claim any rights to this house. 'Manjamma Jogathi mathu Sangadigaru (Manjamma Jogathi and Associates)' is the name under which I have registered my house. All my pendants with figures of Gods will be distributed among them; only what I wear in my ears will be for my brother's family. Of course, my brother says he wants nothing from me, only my well-being. He says they are happy to support me if I need anything.

Even as I pray that no child be disowned for being different, I reiterate that the doors of my house will forever be open to any child who has to leave home for being a transgender, who is disowned and rendered homeless for being different, and who is honest to his inner self.

7

Love in the Life of a Transgender

L ove evades the likes of us. Most men who choose to be with us transgenders usually do so for our earnings. This is the usual story. I too had such experiences that left me both broke and broken and I swore to never fall for a man or to let such thoughts get the better of me.

The first time this happened was in Hagaribommanahalli where I had shifted to from Chilakanahatti when I broke away from Guru Kalavva's group briefly after a tiff. There were two more affairs, but I didn't talk about them anywhere because it always felt like they couldn't be shared because we didn't deserve the privilege of love. But now, when people look at my story as inspirational, hiding this would amount to being unfaithful to the reader. After all, those experiences were important in themselves.

Jogathis cannot openly be romantically involved with men; at least in my time it was seen as wrong. Those who worshipped us would no longer look upon us as possessors of the divine. Our faith and our traditions would be compromised we were deemed to be married; we were thought of as wearing the mangalsutra that

Yellamma wore on being married to Rishi Jamadagni. But we are human, and the woman in us naturally cries to be desired, wishes to be wooed and longs to be loved. It is part of our womanhood that we seek to be desired by a man.

Standing where I do today, knowing full well my responsibility, if any of my daughters sought to get married, I would surely bless the couple. This is not to break norms but only to facilitate inclusive living. Back then, men mostly sought us only in hiding and to feed their fancy. In that context, I am glad society forbade such associations as it only left us wanting, wishful and exploited. For instance, the last person I truly was in love with just left one fine day and I haven't heard of him till date. Apparently he got married and has a family.

I never looked that way ever again. Somehow, it felt wrong, especially given that we are looked at with worshipful eyes as having sacrificed everything to carry the Goddess on our heads and dedicate our lives to Her. This image gets sullied when we live with a man out of marriage. Since the men do not intend to marry nor are there systems that can accommodate such marriages, it is usually a relationship with no strings attached. Most such arrangements are of convenience to the men, but for us transgenders it often arises from a desperate need for the company of the opposite gender and the little pleasure that comes with it.

However, the minute we realize that people's perception of us changes, we tend to put that before our own desires, at least as Jogathis who stick by tradition. The trust that people have in us and our adherence to traditions can't be sacrificed at the altar of our desires. We have the right to seek love but we have a choice to make: between earning the acceptance and respect of society and this.

When I broke away from Kalavva's group for a short while, I rented a place in Hagaribommanahalli, along with two others. It was under their influence that I got involved with a man from a neighbouring village. He was almost seven-eight years younger than me. He had a Bullet motorcycle on which he would take me to temples, the theatre and around town, and that brought me great joy. I felt like we were a proper couple whenever we went to the movies or to restaurants. We must have we watched Dr Rajkumar's *Bandhana* three times! I loved that movie, it was a love story.

But gradually I noticed that people were distancing themselves from me. She doesn't look like a 'Shetra Jogamma', they would mutter. The affair lasted around three years but it began to earn me a bad name. As often happened, he started drinking and taking away my earnings. I found myself trading the rice and jowar I earned as alms for money and buying good quality rice and jowar to make tasty food for him. The two Jogathis who lived with me encouraged me, while I kept spending on this man. I had never 'bought' love like this before. They kept telling me it was my job to take care of him and keep him happy as he was defying society to be with me. He had chosen me over a wife and family and so I was duty-bound to ensure his happiness.

It was almost as if I was on a guilt trip, whereas the reality was that they were having a good time at my expense. For example, they never cooked. On the other hand, I was a good cook and they ensured I remained trapped in the relationship while they enjoyed my cooking. Meanwhile, I defaulted on six months of rent as my finances got depleted. People began to look down on me and this hurt. That's when I realized I couldn't let this happen. I called curtains on it and though it hurt, it was a relief.

He is still around and gives me a call whenever he comes to Mariammanahalli. We are very cordial to each other but I do not give him access to my life and I keep my distance. Ending that relationship also helped me break away from the Jogathis who, I realized, were only taking me down the wrong track, and get back to Kalavva's group in Gollarahalli.

Blame it on youth, but Cupid struck again. At the time, I was a rage on stage, especially in certain roles. People called me Black Beauty, and my dance segments that were interspersed in the plays were a huge attraction. Thanks to my dances, we made some extra bucks. I also had many admirers. We were in Harappanahalli in 1989, and I was still recovering from the first affair. I had lost money and peace of mind, my reputation was dented, and so I kept to myself.

That was when I noticed a young boy seated in the front row at all our performances. He didn't come up to me, he just sat there and smiled from a distance. That's how it started, as a sweet, unspoken affair from a distance. We only exchanged glances. I kept track of when he would go past our dwelling and ensured I was always sitting outside doing some work, like stitching hooks for my blouses or something like that, so that it was not obvious I was waiting for him. Or I would quickly finish cooking dinner and sit outside in time for him to head that way. I was too scared to talk as the baggage of my recent experience still weighed heavy. Besides, I was afraid my guru would beat me up if she came to know of my antics.

This exchange of stares continued for days until he finally got fed up and one day scribbled something on a chit and dropped it on the street as he passed by our house. I was scared to pick it up, nor could I not pick it up. So I pretended to stroll around and then, pretending to have dropped something, picked up the chit of paper. 'Come to the high school field at 5,' it said, since he knew we had no play that day. Well, this was a new challenge. How was I to go to the high school field that was quite far away from our house? There was no reason for me to be seen around that area, that too in the evening. My heart beat loudly as I kept thinking about what to do.

In the evening, I said I was going to answer nature's call and left with a small pot of water. I walked stealthily to the field. He was waiting, seated below the flagpole, and I trembled as I went towards him. But I was scared and rushed back home. We didn't meet for almost a month after that, only exchanging glances and greetings whenever he passed by. A few weeks later when everyone but three members of our team had gone elsewhere to perform, he dropped another chit. This one said, 'Come to Kusuma Talkies, let's watch the second show today.'

Now, I couldn't accomplish this alone, so I suggested to a person who was with me to go watch a film. Some old film was playing that day. She agreed. Once we reached the theatre and took our seats, I told my friend I would go sit with someone whom I spotted and that I would return to her later. I don't remember what the movie was about, we spent the entire time talking. He left before the movie ended. I felt we had accomplished a brave feat.

As our bond grew stronger, I told him to ensure he won the confidence of my mother, Kalavva. Since he was a regular at our plays, she knew him. He befriended her and slowly began to visit us and spend time talking to us. Since she used to drink, he gifted her bottles; she liked grapes so he brought grapes for her. This helped break the ice. One day, I went to meet him at his place because his brother had gone to the movies. It was quite late in the evening and we were just lying down and talking when his brother walked in. He was furious. He didn't say a word to me but told his brother to first send me home and threatened to tell their parents who lived just round the corner on the same street. My friend tried to pacify his brother but he wouldn't listen.

I was trembling with fear and the incidents of the past began to haunt me. I had erased the shame of the past with great difficulty; now if this news went out, I would bring a bad name to our entire group. I left that night and thankfully the matter stayed under wraps. We hardly met a few times after that since I left for Kallukamba after finishing all our programmes.

That's when he started writing to me, pretending to be a girl in order to avoid suspicion if ever the letters landed in the hands of family members. I was so melodramatic those days. I took Anjali, a part of our team, to a corner once and cried my heart out to her. Then I broke a bangle and with the broken bit, pierced my palm so that blood oozed out. And with those tiny drops of blood I wrote him a letter—just two lines—and drew a heart. I was that depressed.

He responded similarly, writing with blood: 'You aren't the only one who is feeling the pain.' He then began visiting me even when I was in Gollarahalli and people came to know about us. We used to travel to Hospet to watch movies and even took a photograph together.

I had a well-wisher called Chandramma and she was scared that this affair too would leave me in a soup. So she, along with Katti Kalappa from Gollarahalli, decided to ask him to stay away. One day, when he was at a bus stand, she and some others threatened to beat him up if he came to see me again. After that, we met once at Kallukamba when I was at Gandhi maava's place and he came by to stay for two days. But that was the end of it. I don't know what happened but I never met him after that and got no news of him either. I visited Harappanahalli after that but had no news of his whereabouts.

Looking back, I am embarrassed but have no qualms admitting my feelings and behaviour. I still have all those letters, including the chits, for old times' sake, bundled and tucked away in a trunk in Gollarahalli. I hope against hope that some day we will bump into each other and I will show him the letters that I kept as a testimony of my love and its truth.

8
Guru Kalavva

In our culture, a guru is regarded as even higher than the divine because it is he/she who leads an individual towards the divine. While the Goddess Herself may have been the reason for the validation of my existence as a transgender way before our Constitution or the modern world could think of it, it is Kalavva, the personified Yellamma, who made me Parashurama and literally lifted me up from the streets and put me onto the stage.

She has been a catalyst for these possibilities, for life in the face of death, for identity in the sea of anonymity, for making an icon out of an individual. With all her eccentricities, I still adore her. For, as an artist and a mother, she is solely responsible for turning a Manjamma, who would probably have been left seeking alms on the streets, to all that I am today. This journey from pavement to Padma Shri was possible only because she had the heart of a mother.

When I broke off from the group after having slapped her, I realized the importance of a guru. I lost all that I had earned and was almost thrown on the streets again with, as they say, 'not a shirt on my back nor a penny to my name'.

The tiff is a black mark on my conscience. It was around 1989. One evening, when we had all gathered at Kuduthini in Bellary district for a play the following day, Kalavva suddenly started abusing me. I had no clue why. Apparently one of the other Jogathis, Ramakka, had poisoned her mind against me. And as she got more and more intoxicated, she became more and more abusive. When I couldn't take it any longer, I gave her a tight slap.

She pulled at my saree and my thaali broke; the beads fell to the floor. That got me more furious since I had struggled to get that thaali made. I began to hunt for the beads that had fallen down. The fight got nasty but all other Jogathis only stood by and watched. While they were all glad that someone had given it back to her, Ramakka wore a sly smile. She had always tried to paint a negative picture of me because Kalavva was fond of me. That made Ramakka jealous since she had been with Kalavva longer.

The following morning, while all of us went to have a cup of tea, Kalavva broke away to leave for home. We tried to stop her saying we had a play to perform that day, but she declared she would not perform with me. She said I should have remained mum and not dared to hit her. I began to fret. Was I the one who had brought our troupe a bad name? We had been performing regularly in Kuduthini, and a sudden cancellation of the show was absolutely unacceptable. The village elders managed to assuage her feelings. I too pretended to make peace and asked her to join me for a juice at the village fair, purely for fear of our differences affecting our performance that night. She had this great quality of accepting her mistakes. That day too she did so and that cooled the air between us.

We put up a good show that night but as we wrapped up and headed to our respective homes, I said this was my last play with them. 'I can't and don't want to work with Kalavva any more,' I told them. 'She is very petty,' I said and parted ways. I came back to Chilakanatti, packed my bags and left for Kallukhamba to avoid being approached by the team again.

A few months later when people from Ranibennur approached her for the play, she told them I wouldn't be part of the team since I was unwell. But the organizers said they had already publicized the programme with my name, and distributed pamphlets; besides, the locals had previously greatly appreciated our performance. So that one time, since she sent Ningamma Jogathi, someone much more senior to even Kalavva to convince me, and my parents both said I should not disrespect her, I performed. But that was the last time. After that, I broke off all ties with her and relocated to Hagaribommanahalli.

This was the beginning of a self-destructive phase. When you leave a guru's house, you end up in a space that teaches you lessons for a lifetime. I did too. After Ranibennur, I joined two other Jogathis, Chandramma and Dhansingh. They were with one more Jogathi by the name of Geddikeri Chandramma who used to sing and seek alms. The former two belonged to the Lambani tribal community. They sought alms for a living, and lived in a rather indisciplined, reckless manner, staying out late, whereas I always did pooja before setting out. But they were the only company I had and gradually, their ways began to influence me.

Chandramma was the leader of the trio and she had a relationship with a man; she had also set up relationships for the other two. When I joined them, she ensured that I too got into a relationship with a guy much younger than myself. In the earlier chapter, I shared my experiences of love. But this time, it was a phase that brought about my destruction. It ended up leaving me penniless, burdened with loans to repay and homeless. I had no money to even pay rent because of all the spending I did for that man who eventually began avoiding me when I could spend no longer. I was on the streets once again, while the other Jogathis went about their lives. I was abandoned: neither the Jogathis, nor the man I thought was in love with me, bothered about me.

The villagers had started speaking ill of us the moment I started living with that man. My reputation took a further hit and I was left with nothing. Meanwhile, the other Jogathis continued drinking on credit in my name, adding to my pile of loans. I even pledged my earrings for two hundred rupees. That is when it felt like it was the result of a curse for having hit my guru. I vowed to myself to never again disobey, disrespect or hurt my guru, and I have kept my pledge ever since.

It was my good fortune that after all this, when I happened to meet Kalavva and the group at the Harappanahalli fair, she finally agreed to forgive me. On the first day of the fair, when the rest of the group saw how pale and in pain I looked, they tried to convince her to take me back under her wing. At first she refused, saying I deserved what I was going through. 'Let her learn. Only when she knows difficulties will she know life, the value of people and remember everyone, be it parents or a guru, and know their importance. She needs to suffer for only that will drive sense into her head,' she is said to have told them. But by the time they retired for the night, her motherly heart began to beat for me. She told Somakka that she was sorry for not paying heed to their words and began worrying about me.

The very next morning she herself came up to me and spoke kindly. She took me back into her fold and set me up in a house with Somakka. This is where and how I could then get a small government house allotted. It was a hut really, but at least it was a roof above my head, a place of domicile. Thanks to this house I then got a voter ID and the right to vote, although my gender then was identified as female. I also got a ration card and my basic provisions were taken care of. Today, we are officially identified as transgenders.

As I have mentioned earlier, the tiny, beautiful house I have now built in Mariyammanahalli is named after her. That was where she used to live, by a large boulder. In 2000, the government used to give twenty thousand rupees to build four walls, a wall in the centre and a tin sheet roof on top. Even as she was performing thousands of plays and was honoured with the Rajyotsava award, she lived in a hut that I call gode illada gudisilu, a hut without walls. That's all it was—she had dug a trench around it so that rainwater didn't enter her shelter. She had laid four slab stones inside to sleep on. The house was so tiny you couldn't even bend and enter, you had to sit down to get in. Yet she didn't bother, she only cared about her singing and performances.

Then, a senior journalist of *Prajavani*, Gudiyali Nagaraj, who was passionate about folk art and brought many artists to the fore, wrote a piece titled 'Kalavva Jogathi, yelli ninna aramane (Kalavva Jogathi, where is your palace?)' after a famous folk song, '*Yello Jogappa Ninna Aramane*'. The article highlighted her dismal living conditions. That alerted the area's member of legislative assembly (MLA), who rang up the zilla panchayat member, Hemraj Nayak, who is now a former MLA and enquired after Kalavva. Nayak said he had no knowledge of any such person. The MLA rebuked him, saying, 'How can you not know a Rajyotsava awardee in your area?'

Nayak then made enquiries and found out that Kalavva lived just off the highway and landed up at her hut. None of us were around at the time. The MLA instructed that a house be built in fifteen days. But there was no land there, just a large boulder beside which she had built this hut. She had sold off the other small piece of land she had lived on for a small sum. We used to cook and eat outside the hut, in the Anjaneya temple in the village. Nights were a nightmare as drunkards and boys roaming around would bother us when we slept there. This nuisance caught the attention of locals who then complained to the temple authorities; as a result a gate was fixed and kept locked.

That left us with no place to sleep. So we went to the railway station where we faced similar problems, with mosquitoes and other pests. But there was no other place to go. That's when I got the boulder broken down, since that portion of land wasn't in anyone's name. People objected to this saying Kalavva had already signed off all rights to the land she had once held. But I challenged them, arguing that Kalavva had been made to sign while under the influence of liquor and paid a dismal ten thousand rupees. I challenged those who had done this.

Kalavva wanted to give up and find some other place to live, despite my objections. She went off to her son's place saying, 'You fight it out and get back the land the way you deem fit.' Only after we threatened to take legal action was the matter settled; the government house was built there after that.

When we were about to begin work on the house after seven–eight years, the neighbours protested, claiming we had usurped six feet of their land. What had kept them from asking about this all these years? It was only after the panchayat and the police got involved that their abuses and fighting stopped and the matter was sorted out. I have shed countless tears to build my house. My struggles continued even after I had taken charge as head of the Karnataka Folklore Academy. Finally, it was only in 2022 that I was able to complete work on this house, which was initially sanctioned by the government in 2017–18. It now stands as testimony to both our journeys—Kalavva's and mine—with all our struggles and achievements.

Kalavva's life is a tale of one too many twists and turns and tragedies. She had been married, with a child, and her wife was pregnant with their second. At the time, she played some female roles in plays in her village. It was after one such performance that she finally gave in to the voice within. She recalled that it was daybreak when the play had concluded. She felt she could no longer pretend to be a man; the woman in her needed to find expression. She then went and submitted herself to Yellamma. Her family was aghast. She became a Jogathi and left home while the sister who lived with them took care of the wife and child. The second child was a daughter. The wife then went away to live with someone else and had four more sons.

The wife returned after many years but the people back home disowned her. She now sported braided, knotted hair as a symbol of her submission to the Goddess; she had become a Jogamma. After a purification ritual she was welcomed into the community of Jogammas. She too began to seek alms, but she always returned home to the family at the end of day, except when Kalavva was in town. Kalavva didn't even want to see her and their paths didn't cross initially. As days passed they adjusted to being in the same house but they never ever interacted. Any time the wife tried to approach Kalavva, the latter would get abusive. She hated the sight of her former wife and even beat her if she approached her.

Kalavva then took Chornuru Chowdaki Yellappa as her guru, who was a very fine artist and played the chowdaki despite his hands being afflicted with leprosy. Together they would perform the story of Yellamma all night. Gradually the team grew to have six members and began to tour as a troupe. When I joined them, we used to stay for, say, fifteen days in one village and perform in the different lanes of that village each night. We found some place or the other to stay, such as the temple corridors.

Kalavva had strange insecurities. For instance, when we were taking a nap in the afternoon, she would go seeking alms alone. She never shared with us what she collected; instead, she would send it all to her son's house. Nobody refused her because people saw her as Yellamma herself. So, no matter what she asked for, sheep or hen or sarees, nothing was denied to her. She would keep all these things for herself, but we never held that against her because she had given us something that was way more precious. She gave us this art.

For some reason, she had a special regard for me, even after the tiff and my return to her. Kalavva never let me fall at her feet. 'You are Settru Jogamma,' she would say. 'Don't.' The meals in the different villages we visited came from local homes and a Jogathi would be sent to fetch it. But she never sent me. Her reason was that I came from a 'big house', meaning an upper-caste home, and so she didn't want to give me such jobs.

She loved what I cooked and I too always cooked what she liked. She liked rice to be done soft and light like jasmine buds while I preferred them a little less soft, yet I would cook it extra soft for her separately. I lived with her like a daughter for two decades, from 1986 to 2005, and today, it is the fruit of her labour that I reap.

In her last days, she went and lived with her son who didn't care to even give her a decent meal each day. He fed her only jowar porridge. Four of us visited her every Sunday in Hagaribommanahalli when we went there for alms. We would earn something like twenty-five rupees the whole day; we never demanded, we just took what we got. It's different these days. Today, you see a lot of transgenders demanding specific amounts of money even at traffic signals. We took what was given as an offering.

We asked Kalavva to come stay with us but she refused, saying she wouldn't be cremated by her family if she didn't die amongst them. She was afraid her folks wouldn't see her as still belonging to their caste. It angered us to see the state she was in. Her son neither combed her hair nor gave her a bath. He wouldn't even give us oil when we asked. She just lay there, in a corner. We would buy a rupee's worth of oil, then sit down to patiently unknot her hair and comb it. Each time we untangled her hair, she lost clumps of it. We would then all pool in five rupees each and give her some twenty rupees before taking our leave.

Her family was waiting for her to die. Such times are like a reality check about who we call our own. Sometimes, when I feel bad for not having a typical family or children, I remember her fate and thank my stars. She had broken her gold medal into two pieces and sold them off for the marriages of two of her granddaughters. We bought her a saree every year and she would promptly pass it on to her sister or someone else in the family.

My house is home to not just Jogathis who have joined me, but also anyone who doesn't have a shelter—there's an old woman who has been living with me for over fifteen years; a young orphan girl with a child whose husband used to get drunk and abuse her has been living with me for the last few months. Our troupe has ten members, of whom most are out travelling and performing while two-three of us stay at home. My daughter Gowri doesn't go out to seek alms. I ensure that provisions are taken care of. I can't bear to see anyone homeless or orphaned because so many people in my life turned my fate around with their love and acceptance when I was orphaned and homeless.

Kalavva took our art to the remotest villages and every lane in them. I had the good fortune of taking it to performance platforms with her, and of making a name for our troupe and the art. When I joined Kalavva, the team members were all in their fifties, much senior to me. I was the youngest one. Then people started calling us Yellamma and Parashurama after the roles we played. I dressed differently from them, I was the 'city-bred' one. The other Jogathis would just wrap their saree around themselves, some covered their heads and paid no attention to their looks. It was a huge deal at the time to go to a parlour, shape the eyebrows, dress up, wear the pallu neatly folded and pinned up. I never dressed like them. I dressed like girls my age would.

This 'youthful' zest that I brought to the team gave us a much younger audience; many of the educated youth who wouldn't otherwise watch our so-called outmoded traditional performances also came to our shows. The best part was that Kalavva accepted it all. She never refused to learn, accommodate or accept novelty. That also got us a semi-rural crowd and newer audiences, and gradually organizations and institutions began to invite us to perform, thus providing newer platforms and avenues.

Kalavva had made a name. 'Kanchina Kanthada Kalavva (Kallava with a Throat of Bronze)' they used to call her because the quality of her voice was gong-like, with a ripple effect. Her singing, her narration, her performances earned her a huge fan following and the art its connoisseurs. I was fortunate to reap the fruit of all her efforts and hard work. I could harvest what she sowed in the form of dedicating her life to this art.

Whatever I am today, whatever I have received, be it art, fame, position or awards—all are bhikshe or alms that Guru Kalavva has given me. While people easily forget their teachers, not one day have I gone to bed without remembering her and her contribution to my life. It hasn't been all hunky-dory. Our bond has had its share of ups and downs, but that is also what made it even more intimate, like a real mother and daughter.

9

Steering Change

About four decades of this battle for acceptance has not been easy. It has been a paradigm of paradoxes. Yet, it has proved that possibilities are infinite—for change, for growth, for making a difference in your life and that of others like you. My life, in one word, is a testimony to possibilities. Problems appear in life only to show us newer possibilities. And the power of possibilities is to be harnessed to steer change.

As an artist it has been one long journey of exploring newer possibilities. Today, I sit as the head of the Karnataka Folklore Academy and attend sessions where we qualify rural artists and performers when they come seeking government pension. But there was a time when this art form was seen as nothing but a means for transgenders to earn a living in the rural hinterlands. It took a Kalavva to turn it into something that got her the Rajyotsava award and me the Padma Shri. My ankles tell the tale of having carried the burden of this art form for years as Kalavva sang and I danced for days on end, week after week, going from village to village. It has been over three years now since I removed the large brass anklets. But the mark they left on my ankles

131

after wearing them for almost three decades are thick and dark, and the pain makes walking difficult.

Back then, when we performed in the villages, those who invited us were required to get us four strings of bells, among other things. These bells were anklet strips that were tied to the foreheads of buffaloes. We could not afford our own anklets. When we danced, we tapped our feet to the rhythm of the percussion. The sound of the anklets showed that we kept time to the beats. In order for the sound to reach the audience, I would often tie three-four pairs of anklet strips and tap my feet hard and strong. Today my feet fail me but the beauty of the dance was enhanced by the sound of the anklets.

The only accompaniments for our performances are shruthi (pitch) and the chowdaki. That's why the sound of the anklet is important. Nothing matches the joy of the sound of anklets, and audiences respond appreciatively, saying, 'This Jogamma dances so well to the rhythm.' I would dance with such energy that at times the bells would come undone and roll away, much to the displeasure of those who had given them to me in the first place.

Those days, we received about fifty seers (a seer is a little over one kilogramme) of corn or a hundred or hundred and fifty rupees for an all-night performance. The money, when divided, would come to fifteen or so rupees per person. With that kind of money, we couldn't even afford a set of men's clothes for the roles we played.

Often, we would have to borrow clothes from the villagers. We had to save up to buy sarees.

Villagers who couldn't afford to pay but wanted a performance in their lane would promise us a share of their crops. These arrangements were ad hoc; often, the programme would be confirmed for a particular day but the villagers would forget upon reaching home after the day's work. They would start making arrangements when they saw us in their lane in the evening. If some didn't pay, we would hold back the clothes and anklets we had borrowed until the final payments were made. There were times when we moved on to the next village with their things because we had not got paid.

I got my own pair of anklets only when we started doing government programmes. At first only I got bells, since I was the only one who danced. Eventually, as the team grew, we saved up and bought more bells. Now I own five-six pairs.

My earliest memories of sporting anklets was way before I became a Jogathi. I used to buy steel chains with bells that make a tinkling sound and wrap them around my feet. Sometimes I used to pin them to the inside edge of my lungi so that I could hear their sound but no one else would notice.

Today the Jogathi Nritya is performed by non-Jogathis too, especially after being included in the curriculum of folk studies; this is the greatest gift to our struggle, to get it the recognition it deserves. Apart from the story of Renuka Yellamma and Parashurama, we also perform other mythological tales like Badavi Lakkamma, Mohini Bhasmasura, Babruvahana Kalaga, Girija Kalyana. There was always an audience for them.

Sadly, no longer. Another Manjamma can't make a living depending solely on this art form as opportunities have reduced, what with the shrinking rural landscape and the advent of television, smartphones and the internet. Television serials were a big blow as audiences, even in villages, began to prefer being entertained in the comfort of their homes. All-nighters are practically a rarity, with devotion too disappearing at a fast pace. We are no longer worshipped or seen as embodying the divine, as we were earlier.

Another change is that our numbers are shrinking. The last person I initiated was around twelve years ago. This is because society has changed and people in rural areas who are differently oriented immediately leave home and go to towns and cities. Many of their families are unaware of the transition within them. Also, once you become a Jogathi, you have to seek alms. But today, there are very few avenues for this because towns, cities and villages have all changed.

I haven't held the padligi and gone around seeking alms since I became the Folklore Academy president, although I continued doing this even after I had got recognition because that is our tradition. Depending upon our custom, we carry the padligi, or perform with shruthi and chowdaki, or carry the Yellamma pot on the head during our rounds.

The visual landscape will tell you why it is difficult. Gates weren't a thing earlier, nor were the kind of compounds we see today. There were fences, of course, but the doors of houses were easily accessible and so were people. Whichever street we walked down, there would be people sitting around who would see us and invite us with devotion. We were treated with the same respect they would show a real Goddess—people would pour water on our feet, invite us in, show us respect and offer grains and other things.

Today, most houses have been replaced with apartments; small ones have made way for large houses enclosed by tall compound walls with gates guarded by dogs. Often, the door to the house is at a distance from the gate, and is protected by grilles and curtains. If by chance we come across an open door, a child will tell us, '*Illa, mundhak hogri* (No, go on ahead).' Sometimes, an elderly lady may give us a handful of rice. How then can this be a means of survival? Which is why, though there are people who get initiated into the Jogathi tradition, they head to Bombay and take to the hijra way of life.

The other reason is that people no longer wait for consent from parents or convince them like we did. In our days, even if our parents reluctantly accepted the inevitable, they generally made peace with the fact that it is the Goddess's will. But nowadays, those who come out of the closet and meet with resistance or face abuse at the hands of family and friends leave home for cities. Very often, they do not even reveal that they have chosen this way of life. They wear sarees and take to begging, hanging around toll booths and so on, but when they visit home occasionally, they wear shirts and trousers. Some get surgeries done and only then return home to reveal that they have had a change of gender.

Those who take to the Jogathi tradition are very few since it requires adherence to a tradition. Back then it came with an aura of respect but that is slowly vanishing. The clapping of hands and whistling associated with transgenders is a hijra tradition. I have never done that. I don't even know how to clap. We have stuck to our music and our gods.

Many Jogathis have taken to the hijra culture, especially those who want to live in cities so that they have better avenues to earn an income, such as through sex work. When they don't feel comfortable there or wish to return, they come back to our way of life. But if they want to return to the Jogathi tradition, having gone to the hijra way of life, they have to redo the process and get the beads tied again. It is a purification ritual of sorts.

Earlier, though, they were not accepted back in the fold because they were considered unfit to carry the Goddess. For instance, some of them get operated on. Once any part of the body had been altered, it was believed that they were incapable of embodying the

Goddess; they couldn't be part of the pooja, nor could they use the padligi. My guru would only allow them inside once we were done with our pooja and five Jogathis had eaten; until then they would have to wait outside.

Once I became a senior Jogathi, I slowly did away with this. I feel we are all one and have to be as inclusive as possible to strengthen our community. We no longer discriminate between 'them' and 'us'. Making outcasts of those who leave the tradition is like undermining our own battle and makes us no different from the rest of society where we seek acceptance.

In this context, I must say the rest of the LGBTQIA community looks up to us in a worshipful fashion, although some object to our traditional way of life and say we need to give it all up if we need to fight for our rights. My argument has been that we need to win our rights even as we preserve, protect and promote our unique cultural identity. Only a few among them made a noise when I did drishti for the President. Most of them realized it was a genuine gesture and were glad because the intention was good: the President's well-being. This is the wealth our culture has given us—nobility of intent and wishing everyone well through every act and ritual. And that is the more organic activism for love and respect, which be much more powerful than legislation to ensure acceptance and inclusive growth.

Activists can go around giving lectures but lectures alone do nothing. They can say what they feel but that day in my saree veil I had managed to touch the hearts of millions across the world. This can't be faked, taught or acquired—this is cultural inheritance. But how will those who sport the saree for selfish, award-winning activism know what these cultural symbols mean to us? For them it may be a costume that brings them fame, attention, but we never can think that way. We haven't donned these clothes or held the chowdaki to win awards, they make us who we are and so we are and will remain proud of every bit of our cultural heritage.

Awards have come our way because the art has found acceptance and audience, and the system has people who genuinely recognize and respect it. Never have we lobbied, nor could we afford to, which is why I always say that it is plain, relentless pursuit of my art that has, in one lifetime, done what activism may not have been able to over many.

My first tryst with honour came at the Sanduru Sahitya Sammelana, where the organizers felicitated me after our performance. Kalavva was mighty upset as she didn't like any of us juniors receiving such respect. It was just her nature. I have learnt from her behaviour and have never envied those who came after me or learnt the art from me. On the contrary, I have recommended the names of fellow Jogathis for awards and honours. I spent half the amount from the cash that came with the Rajyotsava award to make Lakshmi pendants for eight fellow Jogathis and bought two pairs of earrings for two others who were very poor. We then had a feast at home.

The Rajyotsava award was followed by an array of honours: the H.L. Nagegowda award, the S.C. Mallaiah Tayamma endowment award instituted by Karnataka's former chief minister S.M. Krishna in memory of his parents, the Sandesha Kala award, our Aryavaishya community's Wah Re Wah award, the Rangabhumi award, and many more.

The Karnataka government has also been very supportive; it gave me the Kittur Rani Chennamma award in 2019. I have lost count now of the awards I have received and there was actually no space left in the small house I lived in to display them. Just when my term as a member of the Folklore Academy was nearing completion, the government chose me to head the academy—the first ever transgender individual to be made president of a state folklore academy.

While there is some concern that our art has vanished from the streets and become a stage art, I am glad that it is no longer taboo and is pursued by all, irrespective of gender. Those who pursue the art today do it with reverence and grace.

At one time, we were the only troupe of male Jogathis. Kalavva was the first transgender to sport make-up and act in a play. Not many were sporting enough to accept us as part of their theatre production. That is when theatre artists Nagarathnamma and Ilkal Umarani decided to give us a chance and made us part of their *Mohini Bhasmasura* production. We had to unlearn a lot to adapt to traditional theatre as the stage was different and so too the medium. But they taught us with love and that marked the beginning of our foray into theatre.

Accepting us as artists beyond our gender identity was not easy. I remember, when in Gollarahalli, I had once expressed the desire to perform in a play and people had agreed to the request. But a few days prior to the performance, the village elders came to me and said I could not be part of the play because it was a bad omen for me to be acting. They said the neighbouring villagers were also asking if the village lacked men that they had to now resort to getting 'male transgenders' to perform male parts. This taunt upset the boys, who said they would not act with a transgender. It shattered me to hear those words in the village I had made my home. I didn't step out of my house for two days and did not take part in any village function for the next two years for fear of being disqualified from attending for being a transgender.

Those were the days when we faced such dilemmas everywhere. If I wanted to answer nature's call, the gents' washroom was not to be used and the ladies' one was inaccessible. 'Hey Manju, you shouldn't use this one any more, go to the ladies',' the boys would remark. If I headed to the women's toilet, the women would prohibit my entry. Pingponged this way, I'd stand weeping between two washrooms, lamenting my fate. Even to pee, I had nowhere to go. It broke me to know that I would have to go far away in some fields or deserted place so no one would have an issue with my presence.

And that was just the beginning. If I boarded a bus and took a seat, no one would sit beside me and the seat would remain unoccupied. People did not mind standing but wouldn't take the seat next to me. If it was a three-seater, people would leave one space in between and sit at a distance. Even if some did make a brave attempt and sit beside me, they would shrink away and sit uptight to avoid touching me. Whenever I noticed such behaviour I would move out and sit in front so they could be at ease.

Those bruises hurt for a long time, since they kept recurring. There were just a few buses plying in the villages. If I boarded a packed bus, the conductor would keep screaming 'move forward, move forward' and nudging people to move. But if I moved a little the person in front would move far ahead, leaving almost an arm's distance and if I turned back to look, the ones behind me would also move at least an arm's distance. When alighting, those ahead would hurry to exit while those behind would wait a little distance away. These incidents hurt no end.

The government called us 'mangalamukhiyaru' or the auspicious ones; this nomenclature helped shed the air of 'inauspiciousness' around us when Nagarathnamma chose us to be part of her play. Similarly, there have been many changes among the wider folk art community and the environment as far as transgender artists are concerned. Earlier, even after finding space among folk artists, there would actually be no provisions for our inclusion. For instance, at folk art festivals, there would be separate spaces earmarked for male troupes and female troupes, but none for us. That always put us in a fix. We never got any separate rooms like the 'bigger' and more popular singers and dancers did, but even in large common areas like a community hall, we struggled to find a corner to settle into. There were times when we would take showers at midnight, as in the daytime the ladies' and gents' bathrooms and toilets would be inaccessible to us.

I remember once we were in a large room also occupied by some female Veeragase—a traditional folk dance form from Karnataka—artists. They wanted to change their clothes but were uncomfortable because of our presence. We were getting our make-up done. The organizers had put us together, grouping us all as women. But those girls were visibly uneasy. They finally requested us to step out so that they could change.

'Why can you not change when we are around?' asked Yelavva Jogathi from our troupe, who had been in Mumbai earlier. 'No we won't because you are men,' said the girl. 'Who said we are men? We are also like you,' said Yelavva and lifted her saree. The girl broke down and just sat there. She didn't change although the other girls apologized to us as we finished our make-up and left the room.

We faced such problems everywhere. I have tried addressing many issues after I became president. Simple things like arranging lunch for artists who arrive in order to qualify for the monthly pension provided by the government can make a lot of difference to their lives. Most folk artists are from really poor backgrounds and often travel to Bengaluru from far-flung villages. I know what it is to wait for a whole day on an empty stomach while invigilators treat themselves to tea and snacks. Now, every artist is provided lunch unless they leave before lunch time. It doesn't just save them a few rupees, it is an acknowledgement of their presence.

Little changes in the way we accept and accommodate fellow humans can go a long way in making our society more positive and reduce friction. When Chornuru Kotrappa was assistant director of the Kannada Culture Department, for the first time he ensured our art got recognition and gave me an opportunity to teach it to students under the guru-shishya tradition. A stipend of five hundred rupees was provided to the ten students who trained under me. I got an honorarium of two thousand rupees, most of which was spent on the students themselves. He was also responsible for us getting a chance to perform in various districts in the state. Until then, we were not considered artists by the department. I used to tell students how we would give our lives to our gurus to learn for years together, and we always gave them guru dakshina, the guru's fees. Now, the government was giving 'shishya vetana', student salary. I told them they should make the best of this opportunity.

There have been various organizations and forums in recent years that have treated us on a par with others, recognized us as folk artists and taken care of our needs. Such equal treatment facilitates dialogue and mutual respect. I have also tried to initiate changes in the lives of Jogathis who have come to me in recent years by ensuring they obtain at least a basic education. Most of us lost out on a lot of opportunities owing to lack of literacy and education. Even as I push for the government to create more employment opportunities, I also encourage our folk to qualify for the same.

A few years ago, a young boy, Muthu, whom I mistook to be a girl initially, said he wished to stay with us. His sister was married into a family in Mariammanahalli so he used to visit our village. He kept coming home with my daughter Gowri who later told me he was a boy, like one of us. From his looks you really couldn't tell. One day he said he wished to stay back with us and not go home. I said he could, provided he obeyed my conditions, the first of which was that he go back to school and complete his education. He agreed. We got him re-admitted after his parents consented to his living with us. He studied up to Class 7. But then he lost his father and so he went home and never returned.

People say he can be seen loitering around temples. It's sad to see this. I had wanted him was to get educated so he could be independent and have opportunities, but that didn't happen. He would have been in Class 12 had he continued. He roams around in shirt and trousers but he's also had the beads tied and wears all those ritualistic chains, is what I've been told. Recently, when some of my daughters visited Huligi, he performed with them, they said. But he has not returned to me. He fears I will admonish him for not keeping his word.

Way back in 1986, when I was in Chilakanahatti, a few girls had matted hair, which in our region is believed to be a mark of the Goddess. However, by then I had realized that the hair had nothing to do with the divine, it was an infection. So, I sat the families down and explained all this to them and took them to the Huligemma shrine to make an offering. Once shaved and healed, they began to lead normal lives. They got married and now live with their families. Else, the girls would have become devadasis, married to the deity and belonging to the temple. Now, whenever they meet me, they thank me for saving them. 'Else we would have become a Jogamma like you,' they say. It feels so wonderful to know that I could help them start life afresh.

There are many such instances, but I wish they were systemic. I have been appealing to the government for a shelter that can serve as a residential-cum-training centre for transgenders, and that they be provided identification documents based on self-declaration and not have to be registered with any organization. The educated ones then can be provided some basic employment depending on age and qualification, while the younger ones could have access to basic education. Some form of reservation for transgenders will surely enable them to earn a decent living. The decision by the Karnataka government to reserve 1 per cent for transgenders in all recruitments to the police service is a welcome step.

Proactive and empathetic assimilation into the social system will reduce the number of transgenders at toll booths and elsewhere. Why would we want to beg if we are also seen as 'normal' and part of common society, and have the means to earn a decent living and lead a respectable life? There should be old-age homes for transgenders too. At present there is nowhere an aged transgender person can go to, since the regular places will not take them. That would spare them the horror of being ill-treated by their biological families at the end of their lives.

My battle for my community will go on till my last breath as there is a lot to be done and none of it is easy. But I am also proud and glad that I have been able to initiate changes. Of course, it has not been a red-carpet journey. Until a few years ago, there were days I would curse myself for having pursued this art and struggled all my life, while those who had renounced the tradition lived a much grander life. But I didn't give up because each time my parents' words and Kalavva's struggle would flash before my eyes. All the perseverance, patience and painstaking pursuit paid off when the government made me a member of the Karnataka Folklore Academy and then went on to give me the top post. This was something I hadn't even dreamt of.

I had just completed two years of my term as a member and the government had changed, which meant our term at the academy too had ended. It was unimaginable that not just did our region get representation, which it had never thus far, but a transgender artist was holding the top post. Also, until now, of the thirteen people who had held this post, only two past presidents had been folk artists themselves—Picchalli Srinivas and Takappa. While folk artists across the state have expressed their pride and joy upon my appointment as president, some scholars responded with cynicism, and some even resigned from membership of the academy. A well-known folklorist and scholar from Mysuru wrote in his resignation letter: 'Awards, pensions, houses, programmes are all fine. But to give [her] the top post of the academy isn't.' Others are said to have asked, 'What does a transgender folk artist know about administration that they have made her the president?'

Well, if in this day and age, at this level of education and understanding, this is the level of acceptance and inclusiveness, is it surprising that our community feels outcast even now? But then, I have to also admit that others who are now part of the academy, including our staff and the registrar, have been very warm towards me and my leadership, and we have worked like a family in the last two years. There are members who are much more experienced in various fields than me, yet not for a day have they had any qualms about me sitting on this chair.

I sift through all the applications of artists who seek pension and in a matter of minutes can decide if they represent a folk art or not. Many others would not be able to make out if the applications were genuine or not. I am able to do so because of organic indigenous wisdom. Moreover, scholars who dare deny our experience and expertise should know that their academic pursuit is fuelled by our existence, and not the other way around.

As my term comes to an end this year, I am glad I have been able to steer the changes I wished to. Scholars raise the issue that not enough books have been published. Maybe. But what we have done in the last two years has made a lot of folk artists happy. In every district there will be artists who have not have qualified for the awards the academy gives, some may have not made it, some may not even have known how to try. But we have made sure to make enquiries from local sources and honour such artists with a shawl, memento and small purse, wherever we have held events. I have witnessed tears flowing down the wrinkled cheeks of those who never imagined they would be so honoured. For me, that is a far greater reward than any scholarly comment on my performance as president.

When I was promoted to be the registrar and joined the Karnataka Folk Academy, Matha B. Manjamma Jogathi had taken charge as the president. When I first met her, I was a little scared upon seeing her huge personality. But as we spoke, in less than five minutes, she had become 'amma' to me.

In all her work at the academy, transparency has been her key trait. She shares a very close and personal relationship with all the members and staff. The Padma Shri award has not changed her one bit. And it is this simplicity and humility of hers which makes her one among the people wherever she goes.

I am especially grateful to her to this day for all the motherly love and concern she has shown every time we travelled together for academy work or programmes. It shall be a matter of pride for me all my life that I worked with Matha Manjamma Jogathi for three years. I bow down to her for her relentless efforts, her enthusiasm for life and the stature she has achieved.

—*N. Namratha*
Registrar, Karnataka Folk Academy

10

Life, Death and All Else
In Between

Each day, when I wake up and see this body of Manju turn into this life called Manjamma, I realize that the transformation has been the least difficult part of the journey. What followed and remains an ongoing battle to this day is the struggle for inclusive acceptance. Acceptance that isn't an act of tokenism or forced but is organic and evolves with a sense of respect for the life within each of us and the wonder that is creation.

Most families of people like us, distanced or not, are glad to accept all that we bring home. We are allowed the privilege of feeling wanted by our near and dear ones only so long as we bear them some goods or services in terms of income, support or pride. The saddest, most inhumane aspect of this underlying lack of inclusiveness is the way in which the families handle our death. It is heartbreaking to see those who have fed off your blood and sweat wait not a moment before discarding you like grime that needs to merge as quickly as possible with the soil. It is even more painful when they do not even volunteer to give you the luxury of decency in death. I have mentioned how Kalavva was treated by her son even after she literally gave him all that she earned. She did not once buy us a cup of tea, she hoarded every extra thing she collected to pamper this son who in her last days was simply waiting for her to die.

Our bodies go through a lot because of the life we lead, lack of nutrition and care, and the trauma of uncertainty which is a constant. After struggling to survive through what society puts us through, ill health is a given. That makes us struggle to die, more often than not. Sadly, this struggle doesn't end with death. I have seen countless instances when the moment a Jogathi is dead, she is orphaned once again. By the same people she tried to win over all through life by giving them all she could. Those who gladly accepted all that you stocked their homes with and didn't have an ounce of guilt over spending what you earned, those who didn't care if you slept around to earn that money or begged on the streets, suddenly find your choices in life shameful and your existence itself derogatory. 'Leave all that you have been and come back into the community,' suggested the family of one Jogathi called Tuppada Kudike Jogamma, who was Husen Saab before he became a Jogathi. She lived in a predominantly Muslim area. The family wanted that she should 'return to their religion' in her last days but since that was not to be, when she died they sent word for us.

Even among Hindus no one touches the body of a Jogathi until fellow Jogathis first give a ritualistic bath. Most often than not, any piece of jewellery on the body or any valuables they owned is taken off them by their families. But the body itself is not really 'owned' by the family. It is even more distressing when the Jogathis belong to a different religion. They are then disowned at death on the additional grounds of religion which, in my view, is a banal excuse given by those who lack basic compassion.

Tuppada Kudike Jogamma was very beautiful and could give the heroines of the day a run for their money. She loved to dress well and wrapped the saree with a lot of grace. She faced the wrath of her family for getting the beads tied and submitting herself to the Goddess. But she braved it all and even built a small temple on her land. This infuriated the family and the community that a temple now stood in their area. They also took objection to her wearing the saree and forced her to get back to wearing the shirt and dhoti. She somehow gave up the saree but would weep each time someone asked her why she didn't dress up like the rest of us.

They even went to the extent of changing the land records to bring down the temple. But Kudike Jogamma went to court and fought for her right to worship and won against them. When she finally died, the family gave us a call and said they wanted us to do the final rites. We initially thought it was because they would not be aware of our rituals. But the reality that met us when we reached her house tore me apart. They didn't want to do the final rites as she was no longer Muslim.

This Husen Saab-turned-Jogamma was lying there dead, her soul probably shedding tears over the fact that those who had forced her to not wear the saree under threat of cutting ties had done that anyway once she was gone. Had she known they would disown her even after death, maybe she could have at least had her little moment of joy by wrapping herself in the six yards. The family handed us ten thousand rupees saying she had kept this for her last rites. Strange that religion didn't stop them from taking possession of all her earnings, her possessions, her little jewellery but became an impediment when it came to giving her a decent funeral.

We were around eight of us but we could not carry the body, so we got a vegetable cart and placed it on that. Just as we were heading to the burial ground after conducting all the rituals, Hindus who were there asked us where we were taking the body. When we said it was to the Hindu burial ground, the entire group turned on us furiously and said they wouldn't let a Muslim be buried in their burial ground; they said we should go to a Muslim graveyard. The two groups then began to argue, each denying us six feet of earth to lay the body in.

Cast out in life, is this the death that awaits us, I began to wonder. I was ashamed at the collapse of humanity in everyone. My fury got the better of me and I told them I would go leave the body at the bus stand. When it began to rot and stink the municipal authorities would dump it the way they wished to, I yelled. 'Did we ask for this life? Are only Hindus entitled to be this way if life makes them transgenders? She worshipped

Yellamma and fought for her right to do so. Where were you folks then? Where was your sense of dharma then? Why didn't you tell her then that your Hindu Goddess probably doesn't like a Muslim worshipping her? If you want me to dump her body, I will. If that is her fate, so be it,' I muttered in disgust. Then we walked away.

That got the Hindus who had gathered around to discuss and ruminate over what I had said. They realized that they owed the woman at least a decent funeral for having led a life of worship and ritual, and battling it out with her own siblings to pray to Yellamma. My anger was not out of hurt, it was out of the disrespect to the truth. The truth was that Jogamma had given her all to worship the Goddess and all we sought in return was a space for her body to merge with the soil.

Guilt got them all feeling sorry. They came to me and accepted that I was right. They then got together and arranged for a good final procession for Jogamma. They called for the band, volunteered to carry the body and a few hundred people gathered and conducted the rituals with us. Thus she was laid to rest. A few days later, we saw that a tombstone had come up there with the name 'Husenappa' on it. Even in death, the family was not willing to accept who she had become.

They also handed us the large wooden idol of Yellamma that Jogamma had worshipped. But where were we to keep such a huge idol? We then went one evening and placed it near the village Galiamma temple. As days passed by, people began to assume it was an idol of the temple deity that had strangely manifested itself there and began to worship it. It stands there to this day; we too pay our respects to it. Of course, we know she is Tuppada Kudike Jogamma's Yellamma; our eyes moisten each time we go down memory lane.

This was not the first or the last time Jogammas have had to fight for a decent burial. Nor is it about inter-religious issues. Even among Hindus, families have not wanted to have anything to do with the body of the man who chose to be a woman. A similar incident took place in Danayakanakere and as the fight got intense, the locals reasoned that they wouldn't let me have my way in their village. Both communities kept fighting until a Dalit lady stood up for the dead Jogathi whose name had been Imam Saab earlier and said, 'Let us bury her in my field. Let the Hindus and Muslims keep fighting. She had chosen to carry the Goddess, which means we are to treat her the way we would the Goddess herself.' This punched the people in their guts. It then became an ego issue for the village elders who said we could bury her at the Hindu grounds.

These incidents scarred us but at same time showed us the possibility of bringing a change in people's thinking. Yes, I had to be rude to drive sense into people's heads. And that is something I have done on most occasions. But we made it happen. We chose to stand up for our way of life and slowly we see there is a change.

I am glad that my growth as an artist, as a public figure who has not discarded any bit of the cultural inheritance, now includes being a catalyst. I am glad that I have been able to become an international ambassador of my tradition. While Kalavva fought the battle and passed on the baton to me, I was tasked with the responsibility of bridging the gap between what I have inherited and what I would like to have passed on. The padligi that I hold in my hands reminds me it is possible. Each time we do the padligi-filling ritual, we also light frankincense and chant 'Udho, Udho!' We chant this during any worship ritual of the Goddess. Udho is said to be a clipped form of 'udbhavo' and it means 'rise'. The chant invokes the Goddess to rise and the prayer is that there is a rise in well-being and prosperity where She rises.

'Rise, oh Goddess, rise!' I pray today. 'Rise in every heart that reads this tale or hears of it as acceptance and love, so that no Manju who chooses to be Manjamma has to go through what I did. Udho, udho, udho.'

Appendices

Appendix 1
Flowers Are Us

While all the senior Jogathis around me in Kalavva's group always dressed simply, just the basics, I took care to step out as a vibrant manifestation of the womanhood gifted to me by this tradition. Being born male, the markers of womanhood—the saree, long hair, the bindi, the anklets, the flowers and the bangles, among others, transform us into women with all their feminine graces.

I have never ever stepped out of my house without flowers in my hair. Right from 1985 to this day, I have ensured that flowers are part of this identity called Manjamma. When I was getting ready to receive the

Padma Shri in Delhi, I realized I had no flowers. When I asked those with me to go find me flowers, they didn't return for almost an hour. Eventually they returned with one tiny string of flowers after they had travelled a good ten kilometres in the capital city. They found the flowers outside a temple, and paid around three hundred rupees for them!

Coming from where I do, this was shocking to hear. We usually buy the orange kanakambara, also known as the firecracker flower, which doesn't cost more than ten to twenty rupees. Perhaps flowers are no longer part of the make-up routine of city women. For us, these little things complete our idea of womanhood.

Appendix 2
Widowhood

For a Jogathi, especially one who has taken Yellamma as her Goddess, the absence of bangles, flowers and jewellery signifies widowhood and is observed once a year for a month. We believe that Yellamma becomes a widow around December each year for a few moments. There's a ritual in which she takes off her taali, her nose ring and all other markers of a married woman.

At that time, Jogathis who have accepted Yellamma also take off their bangles and nose rings and anklets. For around four weeks we live like widows. On the chosen date each year when the ritual is held at the temple, we go to a honamakki tree outside the village where a small pit is dug, like for a funeral. We apply cow dung and decorate it with a rangoli, pile up sticks and light a fire. As it burns, we break our bangles in the fire, take off our taalis and symbolically also put five black beads into the fire, wipe off the turmeric and vermillion on our foreheads, fill the pit and close it up. Then we place three stones on it, at the feet, chest and head.

The Jogathis' faces are then washed and covered with veils. Those who have taken them as daughters conduct a ritual of cleansing the 'venom mouth' as it is called when they get home. We give them tea and water and puffed rice. They rinse their mouths, bathe and then enter the home as widows. They stay that way for a month. After that, when the Goddess gets her 'raja muttaide tana' or royal marital status, on the full moon day around January, they become married women again.

There is a tale of a king, Singthaluru Veeranna, who is now deified and worshipped as God, sending all the symbols of a married woman to Yellamma whom he sees as his sister. The Yellamma temple on that day receives a new saree, blouse, turmeric, vermillion, bangles and a nose ring from her maternal home, Singthaluru, and her marital status is reinstated. She is ordained as a 'raja muthaide'. Jogathis celebrate this day either at the temple or by cooking a feast at their own homes and they too wear jewellery and all the markers of a married woman, everything that they had taken off during widowhood. Some of these practices are vanishing with migration to cities and the fading of the traditional way of life.

It is believed that the Goddess's presence and appearance bring well-being and so we Jogathis, as embodiments of that divine power, are seen to possess such vibes. This is why people consider it 'auspicious' if we turn up for any celebration or happy occasion, such as a wedding or birth ceremony.

This is what encouraged factions within the community to exploit this sentiment and demand certain amounts of money by landing up during celebrations. Since most are pushed to living on the money they earn by begging, they tend to demand exorbitant amounts. This can change if the community is productively engaged in an occupation that makes them self-sufficient. I feel fortunate that I didn't have to tread that path and could use art for survival as well as a path to carve out a unique identity for myself.

Acknowledgements

I would like to thank my parents, brother and sisters, my nephew and my entire community. I would also like to thank B.K. Vikram, who has helped us a lot during the writing of this book, and his wife Ramya. Thanks to Harsha as well, for making those countless trips from New Delhi to Bengaluru to Mariyammanahalli and making the effort to meet me wherever I was, and holding those long discussions to render my story in the form of this book.

—*B. Manjamma Jogathi*

Acknowledgements

I would firstly like to thank Amma Manjamma Jogathi for being my strength and the reason for this book to happen. I'd like to thank the entire team at HarperCollins India for standing by this unique tale that the world deserves to know. I also would like to thank my mother, Mangala Bhat, and my mentors Shri Vadiraj-ji, Shri Vasant Kamat, Shri Aravindan Neelakandan, Captain Brijesh Chowta for all the support. I dedicate this book to my brother Raghunandan, who is surely smiling from among the stars. I thank B.K. Vikram for facilitating many of the conversations and sourcing the material required for the book.

—*Harsha Bhat*

About the Authors

Manjamma Jogathi is a Padma Shri awardee and a transgender folk artist. Hailing from the Vijayanagara district in Karnataka, she was the first transwoman to be the president of a government academy in India. Her contribution to the preservation and promotion of Jogathi nritya won her Karnataka's Rajyotsava Award, the state's highest civilian award, in 2010, and the Padma Shri, India's fourth-highest civilian award, in 2021. She has been conferred an honorary doctorate by Sharnbasva University, Kalaburagi. She runs the Padmashri Matha B. Manjamma Jogathi Pratishthana, a trust that works for the upliftment of the trans community in India. She works and speaks extensively on gender equality.

Harsha Bhat is a journalist, linguist, author and content strategist. She writes on culture, heritage, cinema, as well as political lyrics and social media and content strategy. A former senior sub-editor at *Swarajya*, she is a graduate of mass media from St. Xavier's College, Mumbai, and holds a master's degree in linguistics from University of Mumbai.

30 Years *of*

 HarperCollins *Publishers* India

At HarperCollins, we believe in telling the best stories and finding the widest possible readership for our books in every format possible. We started publishing 30 years ago; a great deal has changed since then, but what has remained constant is the passion with which our authors write their books, the love with which readers receive them, and the sheer joy and excitement that we as publishers feel in being a part of the publishing process.

Over the years, we've had the pleasure of publishing some of the finest writing from the subcontinent and around the world, and some of the biggest bestsellers in India's publishing history. Our books and authors have won a phenomenal range of awards, and we ourselves have been named Publisher of the Year the greatest number of times. But nothing has meant more to us than the fact that millions of people have read the books we published, and somewhere, a book of ours might have made a difference.

As we step into our fourth decade, we go back to that one word – a word which has been a driving force for us all these years.

Read.

Harper
Collins

HARPER
PERENNIAL

HARPER
BUSINESS

HARPER
BLACK

हार्पर
हिन्दी

HarperCollins
Children'sBooks

HARPER
DESIGN

HARPER
VANTAGE

Harper
Sport